COVID Broke Our Kids

Scott McIntosh

CONTENTS

Introduction

If you're anything like me, you find solace in watching your kids smile and laugh. In those moments, you breathe a sigh of relief and think to yourself, "We made it! Our kids are okay." Then there are times when you see your kids in public, attend a school event, or hear stories from their school day that leave you shocked and thinking, "Something is wrong. It shouldn't be like this." Later, you might even overhear your child crying alone in their room, and that voice inside your head screams, "My kid is broken! Everything is not okay!"

You're not alone—COVID-19 has broken our children. Not just the virus, but how society has handled the virus, how society handled the shutdowns, and how society gave us the information we needed to make informed decisions for the good of our community. Our response to the COVID-19 virus has broken our kids. But there is hope, and we can help mend our children.

I'm a teacher fortunate enough to work with over 6,000 students every year. I travel to more than 50 middle and elementary schools, engaging with every fifth and sixth grader in my school district. I spend two full days with these students, teaching in small and large group activities, and I interact with them in various settings—from mornings to afternoons, during lunch, and even on the school bus. I see them in various emotional states—relaxed, stressed, excited, tired, scared, frustrated, and exhausted.

In recent years, the most common question I've received from chaperones and fellow educators is, "Is it like this everywhere?" In short, the answer is yes—the pandemic has left its mark on our children. The way society has dealt with Covid broke our kids.

Throughout this time, I've grappled with helping our students readjust to life after the pandemic and have developed some simple yet effective strategies to aid them in this process. While I use the term "broken" to describe their situation, it's merely a simplified response to a complex shift in their lives. Our children are grappling with confusion, forgotten skills, stress, and developmental gaps. I firmly believe they can heal themselves; they possess remarkable resilience and are actively trying to bridge these gaps. But parents and teachers can accelerate their adjustment to post-pandemic life and help mitigate negative consequences. We can be the cast to guide and help heal their broken bones.

I have broken bones many times. I have worn casts. They protect the bones and hold them in place so they can heal in the right direction and shape. When I've broken my collarbones, I didn't wear a cast, just a sling. The sling works, but the amount of protection it offers is minimal. It takes the weight off, but it does not protect the bone like a cast does. I have also broken bones and have been too busy to go to the doctor. The bones heal, they almost always do, but they are crooked, and they still hurt when the pressure changes. As parents we need to decide how involved we are going to be in supporting our children as their wounds heal.

Our children are hurt. As both a teacher and a parent, I am constantly asking myself, "Should I be the sling, the cast, or should I ignore their pain because they seem to be managing it?" I have been all of these for my own children. But right now, my wife and I are choosing to be the cast. We are working hard to be a firm support to guide our daughters. We offer this support in the form of structure, routines, expectations, communication, and activities. However, we also want our daughters to be able to function on their own, so we remove the cast and opt for the sling when we think the danger of a re-break is low. We reduce our structure and support to see if they can meet their expectations.

In the beginning of the pandemic, we were ignoring the initial fractures. I think we were trying so hard to survive we didn't notice our kids were broken. Our daughters had hairline fractures that continued to receive stress. We knew something was wrong, but we did not understand how wrong until the hurt was bubbling over.

This book is an account of my experiences as a teacher and father. I will recount my observations within my school system, addressing the time period from the shutdown of schools to the return of our students. I'll share insights into what has worked for me in my "classrooms," which include the students' classrooms in their school buildings, school cafeterias, my bus, local, state, and national parks, creeks, mountains, and forests. While I acknowledge that every school district faced the same issue, they all handled it differently. I hope you can identify similarities, develop deeper empathy for your children, and find strategies and patience to aid your child's adjustment.

Throughout the book, I'll also recount the struggles my family has faced from the initial lockdown to the 2023-2024 school year. I'll explain how my wife and I have navigated our daughters' struggles over the past few years. We have two daughters: my oldest was in sixth grade when the pandemic began, and my youngest was in fourth grade. In the 2023-2024 school year, they will be entering tenth and eighth grade. This book explains the steps my family and I have taken at home to help our daughters cope with the trauma caused by COVID-19. I'll focus on both significant and minor victories, and I hope my observations help shed light on your own children's challenges.

I am not a doctor, I am not a psychiatrist, I am not a therapist, I am not an expert at child development. I am a teacher, a coach, and a dad. Over the pandemic I have been working my hardest to do the best for my students, my athletes, and family. The ideas in this book are based on my observations, my actions, and the conversations that I have had with my wife, my daughters, my co-workers, and friends. These ideas are ones I have used or am currently using every day. They work, but I tweak them a little every time my students or family need me to. This book is the beginning; I am sure we will be working on this for years to come.

COVID-19 has had a profound impact on our children. It has broken our communities, it has destroyed our safety, it has changed our routines and left us to figure out how to pick up all the pieces and put them back together. This book chronicles my journey, and I hope it provides you with insight, comfort, hope, and ideas to assist you in your own struggles.

Chapter 1
The Theft of a Dream

College was my great reset button. My final year of high school I figured out that I missed out on opportunities because I was scared to try. I had regrets. I also had two dreams: to be a marine biologist and an outdoor educator. I applied to two colleges and got accepted to both, one for environmental marine science and one for outdoor education. Both were smaller colleges. I fell in love with the first college I visited and that was all she wrote. I was going to major in Environmental Marine Science. Attending a small college and having all that regret from high school, I tried to take advantage of every exciting opportunity. I got involved in the outdoor club, the rugby club, and the ice hockey club.

My college was awesome in the way it supported students. It had a freshman orientation program that helped you meet other freshmen, upperclassmen, and professors.

They knew that communities for incoming freshmen were vital to increased retention. This freshman orientation program helped build those communities.

When I got my letter to register for classes there was an application for this special freshman orientation program. This program cost extra, took place in Canada, and required camping equipment. Money was an issue our family often talked about when I was growing up. We had enough to live comfortably, but anytime I asked for something it seemed to cause stress. Maybe I took it too hard, but my mom made me feel bad for asking for things. New shoes were always a hot topic. Horrible clothes that nobody wore were always pushed on my brothers and me. My mom was a real estate agent, a salesperson. She seemed to always be selling us the cheaper version of things. Whenever you asked for something, she made you feel bad.

The greatest example of this was when I was 14. My dad took us to a store to look at skis. This store happened to have rollerblades. I tried them on. I skated around the store forever. They had to pry me out of those skates. I wanted those skates, but they were expensive. It was summer, birthdays and holidays were months away. I didn't even ask for those skates. The following week my dad came home with rollerblades. Completely out of the blue my dad bought me those skates. Talk about Christmas in July, it was one of the greatest gifts ever. I had those skates for years and spent hundreds of hours in them. I played roller hockey every weekend and weeknights when we could find enough guys. They were a life-changing gift.

The night I got those skates, I remember hearing my mom and my dad fight about that gift. The skates were expensive, she was upset, and it sounded like she did not think I deserved those skates. I felt horrible. After that, I always hated asking for anything.

But that freshman orientation program, those two weeks canoeing in Canada, were calling my name. Not only that but it replaced a class every freshman had to take. I was getting a chance to explore the world and I was earning class credit at the same time. I wanted to join this freshman orientation program so much that, after some hesitation, I mustered up the courage to ask my mom.

I thought I was going to get the sales pitch, all the reasons why I did not deserve this, all the reasons I should be happy to just go to school. My mom rocked my world when all she said was, "Yes." I was confused and excited, so I tried to explain that I would also have to buy camping gear and other supplies. She still said, "Yes."

The program began two weeks before school started. Dave Ganoe was in charge of the program, and he was a mastermind at organizing, planning, and mentoring us. He had a reason for everything he did and everything he made us do. He moved with purpose. He moved with intent.

We drove to Canada in school vans. There was a van crew that we traveled with. The van crew was freshmen, upperclassmen and a faculty member or two. At night, we camped, and I shared my tent with another freshman. We spent six days camping and canoeing with our trail crew in

Algonquin, Canada. On the way home they shuffled us into a new van crew. We interacted with everyone.

Dave knew what he was doing. He was building a community of students that trusted each other. I got to meet over 65 freshmen and 24 upperclassmen, not to mention all the staff members. We all had something in common. We all had stories to share. The peer counselors were upperclassmen involved in clubs and sports, and the faculty advisers were from all parts of campus life. The enthusiasm and determination of these leaders was contagious. Dave selected them because they were magnetic. They pulled us in and got us involved in campus life. We felt secure in our friendships, and we had a strong community. This allowed us to figure out who we were and reach our potential.

When classes eventually started, I was comfortable and confident. I had a great friend group and knew lots of people. I belonged. We were also connected to all the alumni that were a part of this experience. It was powerful.

One of these friends worked for a summer camp and it sounded amazing. I wanted that job. During the summer of my sophomore year, I worked at a summer camp and fell in love with teaching. College was showing me that everyone learns differently. Study groups were fascinating. Flash cards, rewriting notes, acronyms, and mnemonic devices were everywhere. I fell in love with learning. While working at the summer camp, I got to share my love of learning with my campers, and I loved their excitement. I knew then that I wanted to become a teacher.

Teaching is so exciting. It is also hard. I have never done anything as hard as teaching and coaching except being a husband and father. I love the challenge. I love connecting the dots. I love learning the why. We were all born with this love of learning. At some point in our lives "Why?" was our favorite question. I love helping struggling learners believe in themselves.

I think that I am a teacher today because most of my teachers failed me. They tried to shove me into a box and teach me in ways that worked for other people. I just don't learn like that. I am slow to understand some things and easily grasp others. I am a visual and tactile learner. I love showing my students that there are many ways to learn. I love to find new methods of teaching and instruction. I love truly new ideas that I have never thought about before, as well as concepts that I wasn't ready to understand when I was first introduced to them.

In college we attended job fairs and participated in interviews. I always had a couple of job offers for some far-off state that I did not want to live in. So, when I had to apply for jobs closer to home, I thought I would get every job I applied for. Unfortunately, I did not get any. I was packing my bags, literally folding my clothes and stuffing them in a suitcase, so I could move to Florida to live closer to my friends when I got a call from my current school system.

They offered me a job at the school for troubled students. This school was "the bad school." Everyone that was kicked out of their home school went to this school. The label "the bad school" is not accurate nor does it do the school staff and students justice. Some of the greatest teachers I have ever known I met at that school. I really enjoyed working with most of those students. They were incredibly smart, but they were in some horrible situations. Those students were survivors.

I was learning how to be a teacher. My mentors were great, and we relied on each other. This is where I learned classroom management. I had to deal with students that didn't want to do anything, with students that didn't trust teachers, and with students that didn't trust each other. I had to build a learning community from the ashes of their old schools. It was hard, but all the teachers worked together. We were a very tight community. We had to be because our jobs were incredibly stressful.

I was young and had endless amounts of energy. I was just happy to have a job. But I was not teaching science as much as I was teaching life skills. At the end of the school year, I applied for other teaching jobs and heard nothing. With the summer approaching, I decided to spend the summer in California working at a summer camp.

I was working a ropes course station 65 feet up a redwood tree, when I got a call from one of the schools I'd applied to in the spring. I had to rappel out of the tree and run a mile to the office to take the call. They offered me a job teaching at my former high school. I was excited and said yes immediately. The next question was when could I get back. I wanted to explore California for a bit, so I said that I had to finish up the camp and then I would be home for the first teacher day. Then they asked if I could help coach football. I said "Yes!" I was so excited I think I would have said yes to anything they asked me.

When I got back, I found out that a couple of friends and an old coach were instrumental in helping me get that teaching job. I stayed at my former high school for 15 years teaching science. I loved it. I coached everything they asked me to: football, wrestling, swimming, and lacrosse. I worked with amazing coaches and amazing teachers, and I learned. I learned from some of the best teachers and coaches I have known. I learned the soft skills that are not taught in college or textbooks. I failed a lot. I have seen the power of the right compliment at the right time and the wrong word at the wrong time. I regret things, but I try to make them right the next time; I try to do better. I have never had the perfect day, but I am still trying to make it happen.

Part 1-Me and My Job.

Twelve years ago my dream job materialized. I transferred to the Outdoor School. That old dream that I pushed aside when I started college reappeared, and I jumped on it. I was finally going to be an outdoor educator. Summer camps were fun and exciting, but they remind me of a picture. Summer camp is a moment in time. Outdoor education is the complete story. It is the big complex ideas woven together to bring understanding. Teaching outdoor school has always been my dream job.

This dream was stolen from me on March 16th, 2020. This was not the only dream that was lost that day. My wife and I were also planning a big trip for our anniversary. This was stolen from us as well. Making a choice to stop following a dream is hard. Having another person make that choice for you is so much worse. March 16th, 2020, our state shut down all schools. Everyone was told to stay home. If everyone is locked inside, what will become of outdoor school? My dream job was dependent on getting our students outside. How could we do our job on a computer? The shutdown was the great unknown. My team had lots of questions. When will we go back to school? What will school look like? Will we still have Outdoor School? What will Outdoor School look like? What are we going to do?

Along with stealing dreams, the shutdown also put many goals on hold. This moment was the great unknown and it made planning future activities tricky. My dreams were stolen. My job was going to change. My anniversary vacation was canceled. I was not a happy camper.

My job was a huge question mark. Instead of throwing in the towel, my team and I created a new version of our job. We found a way to make outdoor school work in the virtual environment. It hurt to know what our students were missing, but we still had our jobs, our program, and hope that one day soon it would return to normal.

In my school district, we are fortunate to have four dedicated outdoor school teachers. Our mission is to teach every fifth and sixth grader within our district, enriching the experiences of their science and social studies lessons with immersive outdoor education. In one school year we will teach students from over 50 schools.

During my time as an outdoor school teacher, I've had the privilege of interacting with approximately 36,000 students (about twice the seating capacity of Madison Square Garden). Over the pandemic I taught over 12,000 students. While this may be a relatively small sample in the grand scheme of the country, it's a substantial number when we consider individual families and teachers. On average, a family of four typically includes two children. Elementary school teachers typically have around 30 students in their class, while middle school teachers often teach five classes of 30 students each, totaling only about 150 students per year and 450 students over three years.

In the 2022-2023 school year, my coworkers and I taught over 6,200 students while organizing over 155 trips. Accompanying us on these field studies are not only teachers but also instructional assistants and parents.

Our day kicks off immediately after the morning announcements conclude. We meet with the students in a spacious area like the cafeteria. For our fifth-grade adventurers, we visit their classrooms. We introduce ourselves and lead them to our bus, embarking on a day filled with explorations of our local parks and history. Throughout the day, we witness our students in various school scenarios – from morning routines and lunchtime to collaborative and independent work, culminating in dismissal.

During these trips, it's almost a guarantee that the accompanying adults will share the same observations: "These kids are insane! They are crazy!" They often pose the same question: "Is it like this everywhere, or is it just our school?" Even outside of our work, people are curious about the impact of COVID-19 on our students. My initial response is that the pandemic "broke" them. It is a short answer to a very complex question. I am usually teaching and supervising students so I don't have the time for a long discussion with parents and teachers. I am just trying to let the adults understand that they are not alone; they are not the only ones. This is happening everywhere.

Now, let's delve into this statement for better clarity. I tend to express myself through metaphors and broad concepts, aiming to establish a foundational understanding that can then be refined.

If we were to dissect the statement "Covid broke our kids," it would be more accurate to say that COVID-19 left our students confused, scared, and frustrated. They need guidance in understanding our shifting expectations. With seven major rule changes in such a short span, they are left grappling with uncertainty. They have lost many skills that are necessary for building relationships and working as part of a group. Not only have they lost hard skills such as raising their hand to talk or asking permission to leave the group, but they have also lost soft skills, people skills. How to treat people with respect, how to have a conversation as a group, how to compromise and share (Long). What they need now is a guidebook or a workbook, a clear map to navigate today's rules and a way to rebuild all those skills that were lost or never taught.

Let's take a moment to reflect on the hectic journey in my school district. In just over a year, we encountered seven significant rule changes, a staggering pace of transformation that has undoubtedly left our young learners in a state of confusion.

The timeline of changes we've experienced is a testament to the resilience of both educators and students:

1. March 16th, 2020: The sudden shutdown marked the beginning of a journey into the unknown.
2. March 30th 2020: Continuation of learning–work was posted online with no required direct instruction and teachers had office hours.
3. August 2020: Virtual learning became our new norm, a seismic shift in how education was delivered.
4. February 18th, 2021: The introduction of hybrid/concurrent learning further challenged us as we navigated teaching both online and in person.
5. August 2021: A return to school, but with masks.
6. August 2022: Finally, a semblance of regular school life returned.
7. August 2023: Back to school with a focus on maintaining structure and building learning communities.

On March 16th, 2020, our school district abruptly closed its doors, giving us a mere two weeks to adapt. In fact, the first decision was to close school for a week. Then it quickly changed to two weeks. By March 30th, 2020, we had started continuation of learning. It was a time when nobody really knew how dire the situation would become. Teachers had a brief window to learn the art of online instruction. We had to tackle major problems in just a few weeks.

Continuation of learning evolved into online learning which lasted until January 2021, when some students returned to school while others continued online. It was during this phase that teachers faced the daunting task of teaching concurrently, managing both online and in-person students simultaneously.

In the 2021-2022 school year, most students came back to school, albeit with masks, creating another adjustment. Late in the school year, masks became optional. Finally, in the 2022-2023 school year, opening day felt somewhat normal. Four major changes, each with a different set of rules, understandably left our kids confused about our expectations. They experienced fear and uncertainty, but they've also shown incredible resilience and awesomeness.

Part 2- Effects on Our Kids

Each of these transitions came with its unique set of expectations. The first three changes felt like we were constructing the plane while flying it, constantly adjusting our expectations as we encountered hurdles. Personally, it often felt like I was in full survival mode, trying to keep up with the rapid shifts.

Now, picture being a child during this whirlwind. Their entire world was in upheaval. They were bombarded with information about a pandemic, the constant fear of illness, restrictions on socializing, and the necessity of wearing masks. School, once a familiar place, morphed into something drastically different. It seemed like just when we were getting comfortable, the rules changed yet again. It's no wonder that our kids felt overwhelmed and uncertain; it's only natural. They are broken.

I firmly believe that they will find their way through this maze of changes, and we, as parents, can play a crucial role in helping them navigate and adapt to these ever-evolving circumstances. Our students may be broken, but broken things can be fixed, and together we will help them emerge stronger and more resilient than ever. But first, we need to recognize the extent of what was taken from them.

We caused the death of every single playground they had. We removed all social contact, covered faces, made them social distance, while plugging them into a screen. We unknowingly gave our kids a social media substitute. Let that thought sink in. Not only did we kill their playgrounds and communities, but we replaced them with a social media substitute.

Amidst all the upheaval at school and the death of the playground, there was another profound change that affected us deeply: we lost all of our communities except our immediate family. Almost overnight, our sense of community vanished as we were instructed to stay indoors, and the world seemed to come to a standstill. No longer could we gather with friends and our children couldn't enjoy playdates with their peers. Isolation became a heavy burden, perhaps the most challenging aspect of it all.

Personally, I missed the camaraderie of conversations with coworkers and friends, and my daughters longed for the days of sleepovers and birthday parties. Even holidays transformed into small, intimate family gatherings. We found ourselves isolated from our extended family, and simple gestures like hugs and handshakes disappeared. We even concealed our smiles behind face coverings.

It's remarkable how much information we convey through these subtle gestures – the unspoken language of emotions and intentions. Understanding and connecting with people became a far greater challenge. And as an adult, I struggled to adapt to these changes. I can only imagine how bewildering it was for our children. Our world had irrevocably changed, and in my concern for the bigger issues, I often overlooked the subtle yet significant struggles my family and students were enduring.

Growing up in the 1970s and 1980s, I often felt like the "dumb kid." It seemed like no one cared about my feelings; they simply assumed that Scott was the least intelligent McIntosh. I was aware of my shortcomings. Reading and writing were and still are a challenge for me. I wasn't as smart as my brothers, I wasn't "the best" and it's from there that my reflective journey always begins: "How can I do better? How can I become smarter?"

However, this personal motivation was not an epiphany that happened overnight. It was a dive to the deepest darkest place inside me. It was going to the bottom of the well and figuring out I had to live there forever. When you hit this place, you are angry at the world. You cannot figure out why everything is so unfair. You hate everyone and everything, including yourself. You get nasty and push everyone away. Eventually the anger and frustration grow into numbness.

Luckily, I had some small wins along the way. In fifth grade, I had a teacher that believed in me. He moved me out of the lowest reading group, talked to me like an adult and told me I was smart. He is still my favorite teacher ever; he changed my life with that sentence. He gave me hope. Then, in seventh grade, I won an award for the best dissections in the science class. Again, hope.

In high school I started to figure it out. Ninth and tenth grade were miserable, I didn't trust most of my classmates and I was mean. But I had a great teacher in eleventh grade. She saw a spark deep inside and she was able to fan it into a flame. I grew confident, I grew regretful. The regret pushed me to try new things, and I grew to accept who I was and the strengths that I had. School changed my life and our kids missed out on almost 3 years of it. Imagine all the small, life-changing comments and interactions our kids missed out on. Holy smokes, that is significant!

My job resembles a bit of the movie Groundhog Day; every other day, I experience a "first day" of school. I have a mere 15 minutes to introduce myself, captivate the students' attention, and set the tone for the day. This affords me the opportunity to adapt and refine my approach repeatedly. I can gauge how students perceive and respond to our interactions, allowing me to adjust our communication accordingly. Over the past three school years, this constant cycle of reflection and adaptation has been an essential part of my teaching philosophy. It has also been an essential part of my success as a teacher. I've diligently reworked my instructional methods, engaged in deep reflection on what's effective, and dedicated myself to reteaching. But the beauty of my job is that I get to try it again in two days. I get to rework my problem areas and try again.

Part 3- Now Is the Time to Reflect

Now I've reached a point where I can take a step back and contemplate the broader picture. I feel safe in my job; I feel like my communities and relationships are rebuilding and reforming. I can now honestly reflect on what I did as a teacher, a dad, and an individual. The summer of 2023 was the first time I was able to take a deep breath and reflect on the pandemic; it was the first time I felt like I could see the big picture.

In this book, I aim to dissect the significant changes that our students and children have experienced and how these transformations have impacted their behavior in the classroom, locker room, and public environments they navigate. I'll also delve into the trends I've observed and my interpretations of these shifts. Additionally, I'll share how my family has coped with these changes and how we continue to work on self-improvement.

My hope is that this will provide you with insights into the challenges our children are confronting, allowing you to identify parallels and realize that you're not alone in this journey. Finally, I'll highlight some small victories – strategies and approaches that have proven effective for my students, athletes, and daughters. I hope that you can discover methods that will work for you and your family, and that my insights will contribute to a faster healing process for your children.

When we break a bone, the doctor puts a cast around it to protect and align the bones. This cast speeds up the recovery. As parents, we can be the cast for our children. We can align them to our values and help them rebuild their skills and communities.

Before we dive into the heart of the book, let me share one story. As a teacher, a parent, and a coach, I constantly adapt my plans based on the information I receive, as do others in these positions. All of us have to make a game-time decision every now and then. We are rushed, we stumble upon an unexpected obstacle, and we have to take in all the information we can as quickly as possible and try to make a good decision. Most of the time, this process serves us well. However, what happens when the information we rely on is incorrect or misleading?

Coaching, to me, represents the purest form of teaching. We practice, play the game, win or lose, and then reflect on the outcome to prepare for the next challenge. The game is in real time. You have to use everything you are taught to win. Not only use it but use it correctly. Witnessing the resilience and success of my athletes has been one of the greatest joys in teaching. It's heartening to observe a student grappling with adversity, giving their all, experiencing setbacks, but persistently trying until they succeed. I love seeing their determination and hard work eventually pay off. They become better athletes and individuals. However, regardless of how passionate I feel about the sport and my athletes, I am occasionally misled by my own assumptions.

This is a common pitfall I've encountered during my years of teaching and coaching. At times, I find myself looking at a student or athlete, and they project an aura of maturity and wisdom beyond their years. I absorb this perception, process it, and begin to treat them as if they were older and more mature. However, this can lead to unexpected consequences, as they may not be emotionally or mentally equipped to handle such expectations. Alternatively, I might mistakenly assume they remember lessons from other classes without requiring a review, which can set them up for failure. It's a case of setting my expectations too high, and my students or athletes end up grappling with the subsequent stress, confusion, and pressures, often resulting in a breakdown.

During my six-year tenure as a wrestling coach, three of which were spent as an assistant coach and three as a head coach, I encountered a striking example of this scenario. Wrestling was my favorite sport to coach at the high school level, and one particular year we had a freshman on the team who appeared far more physically mature than his age. We affectionately nicknamed him "man child," but for the purpose of this story, let's call him Jim. Jim had a full beard and stood very tall; I am almost 6 feet tall, and he seems like a giant in my mind. Jim wore the appearance of a senior. In his freshman year, he wrestled in the 215 lbs weight class. Most freshmen wrestle 135 or below.

During a match, we faced a team that had a hole in their line up at 215lbs. No wrestler. But they did have a formidable opponent in the heavyweight class, just one category above Jim's. In such situations, it's not unusual to shuffle the lineup to secure the best match-ups and maximize team points. At the weigh-ins, the other team's heavyweight wrestler weighed in lighter than expected, leading me to believe that Jim could hold his own against him. My focus was on team points – as long as Jim didn't get pinned, our team would come out ahead. However, I failed to consider Jim's perspective.

In hindsight, if I were a more attentive coach that day, I would have seen Jim for what he was – a freshman, a fourteen-year-old. He was thinking he would not have to wrestle and would get 6 team points. The other team would have to forfeit his weight class. Instead, he found himself going up against a senior, an eighteen-year-old.

Jim was understandably upset and anxious. He did not want to let his team down, and he was afraid. In wrestling you cannot hide. Everyone in the gym is focused on you when it is your match. You are in the spotlight. You show the whole gym your heart and soul. He didn't want to fail, but he entered that situation unprepared mentally and emotionally, and he lost. He looked like a man, but he was still a very young boy trying to figure out who and what he was. He was always very successful at wrestling, and I put him in a situation where he could lose all of that confidence in six minutes or less.

It was entirely my responsibility and I failed Jim. At that time, I was relatively young, our team was doing well, and I overlooked Jim's youth. Witnessing his reaction to the loss was excruciating. I had put him into a situation he wasn't ready for with expectations for him to excel. Instead, he got pinned, flung his headgear across the gym in frustration, and retreated to the locker room where he wept. This incident remains one of my three major regrets during my six years coaching wrestling.

Fortunately, I managed to mend the relationship with Jim, who eventually went on to become a state champion. Nevertheless, in that crucial moment, I failed as a coach because I had failed to truly understand what Jim was going through. I had failed to perceive his reality and acknowledge the emotional toll it could take on him.

The most demanding aspect of both teaching and learning is honest self-reflection. It requires the willingness to step back and critically assess whether what we're doing is truly in the best interest of our children, students, athletes, and ourselves. It's not easy to admit that we can do better, but I've come to see that my strength lies in my ability to reflect and continuously improve.

We find ourselves at this very moment observing our children growing older. We are fully aware that they have spent their entire lives in school, interacting with groups, and navigating various social situations. Now, as life gradually returns to a semblance of normalcy, we hold high hopes for their success. It seems we expect them to not only recall everything from the pre-pandemic era but also to apply it at a remarkably proficient level. It is possible they have never even learned the things we expect them to know.

Consider the scenario of a professional athlete taking a three-year hiatus and then returning to the field, with the crowd anticipating their performance to match, if not surpass, their previous level. Picture pausing a beloved hobby for three years and then resuming it, only to find that everyone in your peer group expects you to be just as skilled as you were three years ago. It seems illogical, unattainable, and unrealistic, yet these are the very expectations we now have for our children.

In the midst of these expectations, we tend to overlook the significant developmental experiences that our children have missed. They have endured periods of isolation from large groups, friend circles, and those social activities they once enjoyed. Consequently, they lack certain social skills and we become puzzled when they struggle to meet our expectations. These challenges are increasingly evident in the news, with concerts being halted because the audience doesn't know how to behave, and moviegoers causing disruptions in theaters due to their unfamiliarity with social norms in larger settings.

Our kids have lost their communities and were given screens to replace real life instruction. Their peers became social media and real-life affirmations were replaced with "likes." We shut down the world, killed all the playgrounds, and turned to technology to help us bridge the gap while Covid ran its course.

The good news is that we can play an instrumental role in helping our children navigate this transition. The great news is we have been doing this since our kids were born. By understanding their current circumstances and acknowledging what they've missed or temporarily forgotten, we can assist them in progressing more rapidly. We can actively contribute to rebuilding the skills they may have lost during this unique period of their lives. Now is the time to reset. Now is the time to take our children back from the screens. Now is the time we, as parents, become the cast that protects the broken bone. Now, more than ever, our kids need us to retrain, reteach, and coach them.

Chapter 2
The Death of the Playground

Growing up in the 1970's and 80's I was often sick. I had severe asthma. I spent a lot of time looking out the window at the kids playing. We had no internet, no cable TV, no smart phones, no computer. Just me and my imagination. I dreamed of being outside and playing with everyone. The playground was an oasis, a dream, a retreat, a place kids got to make the rules.

My brothers and I grew up in a neighborhood that was being built. We lived in a townhouse that was part of a row of townhouses. There was a row of townhomes on each side of our row, forming a "U" around a parking lot with an island of grass and a couple of trees. This parking lot was my first playground.

We would gather in this parking lot late in the day to play games. I am sure everyone's parents were somewhere close by, but I just remember the older kids. They organized games and enforced the rules.

We had so much fun playing together. I remember playing Simon says, tag, and hide and seek. I was part of the group, and it was fun. Growing up I had horrible asthma. If I played too hard, I would end up being rushed to the doctor or worse the hospital. Everyone knew I was the sick kid and they had to be careful with "Scotty."

We all learned so much in that parking lot: how to listen, how to be still, how to read the faces of the older kids, and with those faces their emotions. We even learned how to be fair. The playground was our space. We defined the rules, the game, and we learned how to deal with the world. It was our social experiment. We figured out who had empathy and who had none. We knew who was selfish and who was generous. We were included in small groups and excluded from other small groups.

The playground is where we discovered our first real-life superheroes. I mean, our parents were superheroes, but they were so much more than that. The older kids were our first look into the future. They showed us all what growing up looked like. I wanted to run like them and be cool like them; they were real, and they were bigger, faster, and stronger. They could also be mean in all sorts of creative ways. The older kids were quickly put into two columns: superhero or supervillain.

The really cool thing was that sleep was the big reset button. Tomorrow was a new day and the playground would be there calling our names. The social experiment was reset and we could try again tomorrow. We fought, we played, we got hurt, and we played again. Our playground helped us learn about the world around us and about ourselves. The older kids hit the reset button too. Sometimes their roles would change, superhero today, supervillain tomorrow. We got to watch the older kids interact, watch how they policed our playground, and when things got out of hand, we saw parents swoop in and deal out swift justice. My parents were close; everyone's parents were close. Moms were everyone's mom, and you'd better listen. Hugs and insight were there for the asking.

As we got older, our playgrounds grew in number. We were able to explore our neighborhood with friends. "Stay together, be back before dinner," became the new rule. We discovered swing sets and bike paths. New courts and cul-de-sacs were discovered. Houses and basements of friends were opened up, and we explored and played in them.

Just as we were getting comfortable with our little piece of the world, our family moved. We moved to a split-level house in the newest part of the same development. It was less than a half of a mile from our old house, but it was a world away. The land all around us was under construction. We had a new playground that was changing daily. And a new supervillain: the "Pony Lady."

The Pony Lady drove around and tried to keep us out of the new construction. It was a huge game of cat and mouse. When we lost, it was into the back of the car and a drive to our house. The stern talking-to from our mom was never as bad as the humiliation we felt from getting caught.

After the construction ended, we had new swing sets, ball fields, courts, creeks, and farm fields. Our world and our playgrounds expanded again. We learned how to ride bikes and this act of independence allowed us to explore farther from home. As our distance from home increased, our safety nets fell away. Parents could no longer watch us from the windows, and we were left to deal with the superheroes and villains on our own.

Around this time, my asthma was really getting out of control. It felt like I was inside three times as much as I was outside. Missing a couple days on the playground was tragic. Rules and games changed, small groups formed and re-formed. Social structure had to be learned and re-learned fast. Watching everyone and figuring things out became a life skill. Punishment for not understanding the new rules was usually a fight, verbally or physically, or worse, isolation from the group. To this day, I still like to listen first and observe everything. I like to try and figure out the rules before I play; I don't want to mess up the rules or get isolated from the group.

At the end of third grade, we moved one last time to a very small development. It had single family homes on large lots surrounded by creeks, farms, and a forest. In the whole development, there were fewer than 25 kids. Five families of kids hung out together off and on as we grew and graduated from high school. There were others that would pop in and pop out, but the five families were always our go-to. But the world was changing. Video games like Super Mario appeared, cable TV. showed up, and the bus ride

home was a constant battle to get kids to the playground. Our games had changed to football, baseball, roller hockey, skateboarding, biking, fishing, and exploring the creek.

Our playground was a special place. We learned so much. We failed, we succeeded, we pushed ourselves, and we figured out this world we lived in. We built forts, caught snakes, explored, and discovered teamwork. We lost our minds, threw temper tantrums, and we left with our ball. We saw the impact of our actions and everyone else's. We figured out who we wanted to be like and who we did not want to be like. We discovered ourselves on that playground and on March 16th, 2020, we killed every playground in my state for at least two weeks. We stole all those opportunities, dreams, and interactions from our children.

I think it was important to shut down our state. I think it was the right call. But this decision had a lot of unintended consequences for our children. We are still dealing with these consequences. I see them at work, I feel them in my mental and physical state, I see them impacting my daughters and their friends.

Part 1- Me and My Job

The first person to inform me about the virus was my mom. I paid her a visit around January 2020, and she was livid. She wanted to understand why we were allowing people to enter the United States and spread this virus. At the time, I thought she was crazy. I have a deep love for my mom, but I couldn't help thinking she was being a bit paranoid.

My mom divorced my dad when I was a senior in high school. She was given everything she asked for in the divorce; my dad just wanted out. But if you asked my mom about the settlement, she would say my dad manipulated her and talked her out of his pension. She had thousands of stories that were twisted just enough to give her some sense of being right.

I know that she felt guilty for breaking the family. She would ask about it in the quiet moments between the chaos. She always wanted to know if I forgave her and I always told her the truth, "I just want you to be happy." When her second husband died, my mom gave up. She became self-destructive and abusive. Not always; we had some good moments, but isn't that the method of the abuser? Just enough good to keep hope alive. Then I had kids and I stopped allowing her to abuse me so much. It was all verbal and mental abuse, and my kids gave me the strength to walk away. When I distanced myself from her, she started behaving better, but when she turned on me it was ugly.

I remember going over to her house to set up a new smart TV. In the span of 10 minutes, my mother went through every emotion you could imagine to justify me buying her the TV and setting it up. I was doing this; I was in her house unpacking and setting up her TV. When she started to get mean I told her outright that if she was going to verbally abuse me, I was going to stand up and leave. She stopped, looked at me, laughed and said, "Oh, Scott Michael, I can figure this out, I just don't want to." It was one of the most honest things she had said to me in years. By the time

2020 hit, my brothers and I knew that you could only trust about 10% of what our mother said.

She wasn't crazy, she just wanted pity and I didn't have time to go down that road. I know where it goes, and it usually ended with her calling me a bunch of horrible names and me leaving. So, I chalked it up to mom being crazy; I thought the virus was a lie.

I visited her again in February, and she was still voicing her concerns. I still had not heard anything. Since I hadn't heard about it elsewhere, I continued to dismiss her worries.

In March, I began to finally hear about the virus, and just two weeks later, schools were abruptly shut down. My mom had been right all along. Who would have thought?

On Friday, March 6th, I received an email from work that provided a basic introduction to the Corona virus and outlined measures to protect oneself from the spread of germs. It conveyed that the risk of transmission to students was currently low, but our school system was taking precautions. Essentially, it emphasized coming to school, maintaining hand hygiene, cleaning high-touch areas, practicing good sanitation, and staying home when sick. All I could think was that common sense is not so common. About time they were telling everyone to take care of themselves. I was thinking about the flu. I was thinking about the common cold. I was thinking, "please keep your sick kid home, I don't want to get sick."

Not even a week later, on Thursday, March 12, I received an email announcing that all state schools would be closed from Monday, March 16, to Friday, March 27, with the purpose of preventing the spread of COVID-19.

Of course, I wanted them to close on Friday, March 13th. I was all angry about it. Just close tomorrow. Such a horrible response, I know. Friday, we sat as a team talking. It was one of our transition days to get ready for 6th graders. I remember a bunch of questions with no answers. One of my teammates asked what we were going to do when we got back, and I just said, "We are not going to be back in two weeks." The flu lasts for months. I was sure we were going to be out for at least a month. Little did I know it was going to be almost a year.

On Friday, March 20th, 2020, I received an email outlining the plan for implementing continuity of instruction. This communication included training materials and YouTube lectures that needed to be completed by March 24th. We were tasked with transitioning to standards-based activities and assignments that could be completed with limited instruction, all while students were not physically attending school. This marked a significant upheaval in my professional world.

As a parent, this situation filled me with stress. Hundreds of questions popped into my mind. Will I get paid on the next pay day? When will we go back to school? Is the virus in my state, county, city? What can I do with the two weeks off? What are my kids going to do? What is my wife going to do? What about grandmas and grandpas? What about my mother? Everything was a question. In the first weeks of the shutdown, you had to have a note from your employer to say you could be out and about. It was scary.

Never in my life had I witnessed schools closing due to a virus. While we were familiar with flu seasons and periods of low attendance due to common colds, this was on an entirely different scale.

I've dedicated my life to the study of science, particularly biology. It was one of the subjects I excelled in. I hold degrees in biology, environmental/marine science, and even a master's degree in environmental biology. Throughout my academic journey, we were consistently taught about the impending challenges related to pathogens and disease-causing organisms, especially with the growing population density.

Historical events like the Black Death, Ebola outbreaks, the persistence of Malaria, and even annual flu seasons served as stark reminders of the threat posed by diseases. Among them, airborne pathogens are particularly terrifying. Everything that I heard in the beginning led me to believe that this virus was not airborne. So, when schools shut down, fear gripped me. To cope, I immersed myself in various distractions, diverting my attention away from the anxiety.

My family became the focal point of my life during this period. We embarked on family walks, indulged in game nights, enjoyed movie marathons, and I took on home improvement projects. All the "need to do but don't want to do" things suddenly became important. I rebuilt the shed and redid part of the deck, and my girls painted their rooms.

I cherished all the quality time we spent together and, at times, even felt guilty about how well things were going. I work in the local, state, and national parks; being outside is my wheelhouse. We went hiking almost every day when we were given the green light to be outside. I know a lot of people were stuck inside, wondering what to do. I had a head start, and I used that head start to explore the forests and trails with my family. Our basic needs were secure, we had food, shelter, family, and places to enjoy. I even had a job that was committed to taking care of the students. During the first couple of months, we did well.

Yet my daughters, aged twelve and ten, were on the cusp of their teenage years. They were not really talking about their feelings. I saw lots of smiles. I did not realize the fear and anxiety they had. They were longing for their friends and hurting inside.

I had prior knowledge about the Spanish flu before COVID-19 emerged. I understood that it had taken five years to run its course and that we wouldn't be returning to school in the spring of 2020. Despite this awareness, I remained optimistic. I firmly believe in the resilience of humans, and I hold the conviction that children are even more resilient than adults. I was convinced that our kids would weather the storm just fine, but I was wrong. I had underestimated the profound impact the pandemic would have on our children, and in hindsight, I should have foreseen it.

In addition to losing peer interaction, we also lost our sense of community. These were the places where we found our sense of belonging, such as school, church, the gym, locker rooms, theaters, concerts, clubs — we lost them all. I play ice hockey; the locker room is where we bond. We talk in a language only hockey players understand. We tease and compliment, build each other up and keep each other from getting too full of ourselves. We are working together to be successful, to find our synergy. Then we get to push ourselves to the limit to try and win, to try and be our best. Instant gratification or instant failure, the feedback is instant. To get lost in that community for a couple of hours helps recharge our soul and it makes going to work the next day worth it. Think about your communities. Isn't it so refreshing to talk to someone that understands your passion? We lost all of that instantly.

To compound matters, my school system opted for continuity of instruction, which introduced another set of challenges. My wife and I had to navigate the complexities of new technology to deliver lessons online. We took classes to enhance our skills, collaborated with colleagues, and worked diligently to figure everything out. Our school system did have an evening school and a summer school program that were mostly online before the pandemic. I had experience teaching both of these, and my wife had taught summer school online. We had a big head start on most of the school systems.

I want to make this clear: I am immensely proud of what my school system achieved. I take pride in the work I contributed, and I am grateful for the support and collaboration I received. I'm thankful for the opportunities my daughters had. What my school system accomplished was truly remarkable. However, it came with its fair share of growing pains, and the stress was palpable. I knew that my team was giving our students a fraction of the program we normally delivered. We teach with stories, experiences, and places. I love seeing students' reactions to the landscape and history. They explode with excitement. I love it! I was missing all that personal feedback, and I hated it. I love to weave together ideas and help my students make connections. In the back of my mind, I couldn't help but think about how much my students were missing out on. My lessons were not as good, and that was depressing. Every little win felt better, but it was not the same, and that was also depressing.

Since my wife and I were both educators when schools shut down, we had a slight head start compared to most families with helping our children navigate the continuity of instruction. Still, we were sailing uncharted territory and our daughters had to grapple with adapting to online learning – finding their classes, accessing assignments, submitting their work, and communicating with their teachers.

That spring remains a hazy blur in my memory, but it was a challenge we all had to face together. It was happening so fast. We were all doing what worked for us and every teacher was a little bit different. Nationally, teachers on the cutting edge of technology were running Zoom meetings until they got hacked. Then our school system sent emails that told us Zoom was not to be used by teachers. Our district knew that not all students had the same resources so requiring students to show up to class was not an option. Middle school teachers were supplying about two to three hours of work a day. No direct instruction.

Building the online lessons required a ton of work. The worst part was hearing your own voice in a lesson. We made videos and they were horrible. Then we made them again and added words and special effects, and they still were horrible. Spending hours in front of the computer listening to yourself is a special kind of torture. One day, we decided to add an accent: David Attenborough. Listening to my boss narrate a video with his best impersonation of Attenborough was priceless. We found our fun. The goal was to add our personalities back into the lesson. Easter eggs and inside jokes were scattered throughout our lesson. But the biggest win was background music. When my boss shared his first video with background music, I was shocked. The music tied it all together. I called and needed to know the secret. Then I had to redo every video I made. I wanted to cry and jump for joy all at the same time. It was magic.

My wife and I had to figure out the continuity of instruction for the sake of our jobs, and our children had to figure it out for the sake of their education. Our household became a united front, but it was challenging. I recall hearing countless tales of struggle from friends and coworkers. How do we keep up with students that work fast, how do we reach students with no access? How do we organize our assignments, how do we connect with students?

We left thinking it was going to be two weeks. Many teachers did not get to say goodbye to their students for the summer. Imagine having a student that makes your day practically disappear because they don't have reliable internet. It is very hard to lose students that way. The unknown, not knowing why or how the student is doing, hurts.

For many of our students, the transition seemed insurmountable. My wife talked about students that were in her class that never signed on to get work and never picked it up in the office. Why? Did they need help? Did they have support? You could not help but worry about students that did not partake in continuity of instruction. The worry is stressful, it is draining.

Continuity of instruction brought about a change in the rules for both students and teachers. We made diligent efforts to set clear expectations and adapt them as we progressed. I believe we effectively communicated our expectations to our students and their families, and we approached the situation with empathy. We recognized the need to limit both the scope of expectations and instruction. Student work time was tailored to their respective grade levels, and grading continued as usual. Our primary focus remained on ensuring students had access to lessons and were engaged in the learning process. As teachers, I felt we handled this transition effectively.

My classroom is one of my favorite playgrounds. Learning is fun! It hasn't always been fun, but it started that way. Curiosity and wonder. The question "Why?" Watching my daughters grow up, they love to learn. In my junior and senior year of high school, I rediscovered this joy. In college I embraced it. In my classroom I work to make my students embrace it. I try to make my joy of learning contagious. Learning is fun and my classrooms are my playgrounds. I invite my students to share my playgrounds, and I strive to make learning fun, exciting, and challenging.

I missed my real classrooms, the trail, the creek, the river, the mountain. Once I was done grieving for them, I had a new challenge: I had to make my online classroom as exciting and engaging as my real classrooms. I fell short, but I did make exciting and engaging lessons.

Personally, I approached this challenge with a sense of freshness and enthusiasm after I embraced the change. It took some time to grieve and get all my whining out. But when I accepted my new teaching format, I was determined to make it work, driven by the twin motivators of job security and the desire to ensure students continued to receive quality education.

The nature of our job does not give us time for planning and organizing digital resources. We teach outside. The closest thing we get to digital resources are GPS's and digital probes for testing water chemistry. Everything else is hands on, pencil and paper stuff. We have a website, but it is not a focus; it is an afterthought.

We teach in front of students all day, then we drive the bus back and the day is over. We are either running a trip or we are getting our equipment and classrooms ready for students. We don't have time to work on digital resources.

Every couple of summers we get to work on curriculum. Two or three days working with other teachers. We usually run out of time, throw everything in a folder and give teachers access to it. If the teacher wants to search through all the resources, they can, but it is hard work.

Our first goal was to organize our digital resources and get rid of obsolete documents and activities. Housekeeping! We started by digging through our old and outdated online resources. It was like weeding an overgrown garden. We could see the years of work stacked on top of each other and we dug through that digital pile of documents, pulling out the usable lessons and getting rid of the ones that had become obsolete.

The digital resources are for the teachers to support our lessons. Digging through our online resources helped us realize that they were too hard to find and use. Once we organized our resources, we were not happy with the quality or accessibility. We teach these lessons every day. We are the experts, and we decided that while the lessons were okay, we wanted to make them awesome. We found our purpose.

We had a new goal. My boss and I wanted to make canned lessons for teachers. Usable stand-alone, high-quality lessons that were easy to find and ready to use. Amazing lessons, aligned with the next generation science standards, one click away. This was like removing weeds so we could see the flowers.

These lessons were a shadow of our in-person lessons. Everyone on my team felt the loss. No instant positive feedback. No student reactions. No personal interactions. No playground. My classroom felt like a deserted island, and I was a sailor that was trapped and just wanted to be rescued. Lessons without students. Empty. I became a teacher because the feedback and excitement my students share makes my soul sing. I am sure many of my students felt empty as well. The pandemic stole our opportunities to explore our world and find our place in it. It crushed our hope and killed our playgrounds.

Part 2 - The Changes and Challenges Students Faced

In our roles as educators, we were thrust into a whirlwind of uncertainty. We found ourselves navigating uncharted waters, and our students were right there with us, plunging into the unknown. Some students adapted remarkably well, while others faced greater challenges. Similarly, some families smoothly transitioned into this new reality, while others encountered significant hurdles. My own family grappled with difficulties, though they were comparatively less severe. However, it was the youngest students and their teachers who bore the heaviest burden.

The speed at which we made this transition was truly astounding. We shuttered our physical school doors on March 16th and were ready to provide continuity of instruction by March 30th. In just over two weeks, we completely upended our children's world. We stripped away their sense of community, isolated them from their peers, and introduced them to an entirely new digital learning platform on the fly. School, which once consumed over seven and a half hours of their day, was now condensed to roughly two hours. We effectively dismantled their greatest playground.

This is a profoundly impactful statement. Reflect on all the essential social skills children acquire through playing with others on the playground. Consider the significance of recess, the simple joy of attending physical education classes to learn new games, the challenges of the lunchroom, or the pleasure of hanging out with friends at the park or in the hallways. The playground served as a school of its own, where children discovered and adhered to its unwritten rules, learning how to navigate both small and large group dynamics. All of this was abruptly taken away from our children in the blink of an eye.

In the beginning, our community largely embraced these changes. Most people earnestly tried their best to adapt. There were a few who resisted, but by and large, we watched as the number of COVID-19 cases continued to rise. We began hearing about people we knew falling ill. The decision to shut down the playground was deemed essential to safeguard the health of all. However, it was not just one playground that was closed; we effectively shuttered every type of playground, both official and unofficial. After-school activities, sports, clubs, bands, restaurants, concerts, plays, parks, and even national parks—all were simultaneously brought to a halt.

This marked our first significant transition, and to me, it appeared to be the easiest. We were all willing to lend a hand and make improvements. Fear was prevalent, but it was coupled with a sense of freshness. None of us knew what lay ahead, but we had successfully initiated the first change and rewrote our rules. I think we all had a sense of hope. Do this now, do it well, and in a month or two everything will be normal.

Our children had to adapt to this new set of guidelines, and it marked the beginning of a gradual breakdown in their accustomed routine. We had altered the structure of learning, a necessary step, but not without its costs. We sacrificed our communities to protect them. Shut them down now so we can enjoy them later. It also marked the onset of mounting stress. I believe we handled it well, but the uncertainty of what was to come and when it would end hung over us.

Once more, our resilient children rolled with the changes and transitioned to online learning. I have vivid memories of my girls sitting at the kitchen table, fully engrossed in their schoolwork on our Chromebook. Our youngest was in fourth grade and was required to dedicate about an hour and a half to schoolwork, while our oldest daughter was in 6th grade and was supposed to allocate around two and a half hours.

We had established a new framework, and our students understood their expectations. Although I don't think anyone particularly enjoyed it, we were all committed to making it work. We were fully invested. If this had been the only major change, I believe everyone would have coped reasonably well. Personally, I think everyone was in survival mode, concentrating on the next day and week. Thinking about the months or years ahead was beyond my capacity at the time. I was simply holding on and striving to maximize the situation, and my children were doing the same.

On April 17th, the state made the decision to keep schools closed until May 15th. For me, this brought a sense of relief. Establishing a routine can be challenging, but once you're in it, change can be even harder. I simply wanted more time to focus on improving the situation, believing that more time would yield better results. I know that not every student or family felt this way. Parents wanted to get back to work and they wanted their kids in school.

By April 28th, all sports were canceled for the remainder of the school year, and this news weighed heavily on our community, especially the high school seniors. Despite the decision being data-driven, it seemed to extinguish everyone's hope, and families rebelled against it. The pandemic had taken away unique opportunities our kids could never reclaim. As a community, we felt helpless watching our children suffer as the disease continued to spread.

Part 3 - How My Family Reacted and Adapted

Initially, my daughters were a mix of excitement and sadness. Two weeks off from school sounded like a dream, but they also felt a sense of longing for their friends as fear hung in the air. My eldest worried about boredom, pondering how to fill two weeks. Looking back now, we share a chuckle at the thought, considering it ended up being months and months. On the other hand, my youngest was simply thrilled at the prospect of two weeks off of school.

I believe our family fared quite well in the initial weeks of the pandemic. To stay active, we bought our girls new bikes and immersed ourselves in outdoor activities, taking numerous walks and hikes. We also embarked on projects like painting the girls' bedrooms and participated in activities like displaying stuffed animals in our windows, decorating our driveway with sidewalk chalk, playing board games, and even binge-watching "Survivor." As we watched the news, we came together as a family, witnessing the world grappling with the deepening pandemic.

Those early days filled with precious family time are something I'm genuinely grateful for. We got to slow down and enjoy each other. Usually, we take a summer adventure with just us. We explored, hiked, took care of the house, and enjoyed each other's company. This felt like a prolonged summer. I enjoyed it. However, my wife and I were acutely aware that our daughters were missing out on essential experiences.

This was a pivotal moment in their lives, marked by transformation and growth. It was a phase when they should have been investing energy in nurturing their own social lives. However, instead of fostering their friendships, we enforced social distancing. We effectively killed the playground. All of them all at once. We suspended sports activities, curtailed social gatherings, stopped shows, and stopped church. We shut down every community that we belonged to except our immediate family. We inadvertently created a social void, and to compound matters, my daughters didn't have social media. Meanwhile, many of their peers turned to social media to cope with the sudden social vacuum. My daughters missed their friends. They wanted phones and social media, but we were not ready to open that door.

As parents, we focused on keeping our kids engaged and occupied. After careful deliberation, my wife and I made a collective decision that it was finally time to welcome a puppy into our family. I had reservations about it, but I had run out of excuses. We had the time, and the world was effectively shut down. Both of us believed that a puppy would serve as a much-needed distraction with numerous benefits.

Our decision to bring a dog into our lives was a significant triumph. However, the process of finding the right dog posed its own set of challenges. Shelters had closed their doors, unresponsive to emails or requests. Eventually, in April, my wife stumbled upon a dog on Facebook, and our journey to become pet owners commenced.

As educators, both of us were determined to involve our daughters in the dog's training. The dog was meant to be a source of distraction and provide experiences that our girls were missing out on. Dog training, we knew, would instill responsibility and leadership skills. We hoped that the dog would instill purpose and motivation in our daughters. Remarkably, the dog also helped us become a part of a new community. At a time when many were losing their sense of community, we found a way to become members of a brand-new one—the community of pet owners and dog trainers.

As a teacher, I instantly recognized the parallels between teaching students and training a pet. In the first week of school, you aim to get to know your students, establish routines and structure, and communicate your expectations clearly. Training a dog involves minimizing distractions, maintaining clear communication, and adhering to a consistent routine. Your pet needs to understand its role in the family, grasp the structure of the pack, and be aware of your expectations. Luna, our dog, was a true blessing and played a pivotal role in helping our family navigate through the challenges of the pandemic.

Bedtime transformed into a time for dog-related books and learning from Cesar Millan, while free time became an opportunity for us to explore instructional videos by Zak George on YouTube. As parents, my wife and I shared a new purpose: we wanted our daughters to be involved and responsible for Luna. Luna was meant to be a cherished family pet, not just mine or my wife's. This shared responsibility invigorated us. It provided us with a renewed sense of purpose and hope. Our dog became the motivation we needed to navigate the spring and savor the summer.

On April 15th, 2020, our state mandated the use of masks indoors and outdoors when social distancing was not feasible. We made an effort to spend as much time outdoors as possible, exploring the woods, creeks, rivers, and mountains, which became our new playground.

When our state announced on May 6th that they had made the decision to keep schools closed for the remainder of the year, I found myself relieved. I was settling into a rhythm at work and cherishing the time spent with my family. My enduring optimism persisted because I knew how resilient humans can be. However, my wife held a different perspective. She shared a Facebook post at the time that, in retrospect, contained significant foreshadowing.

May 7, 2020 · 👥

For mothers day and my birthday (less than a month away), I want (in no particular order):

🧍🧍😆 My children to find a way to connect meaningfully with friends and not be sad

🐚🥏✏️ My students to be at peace and not to see school as a pointless chore as it continues online

📖 No more bad news in my inbox

🔨🔧🏔️ A day of temporary amnesia, weather that's sunny but not hot, and lots of energy to tackle projects around the house

And if those emojis aren't showing up for you, you're really missing out. 😂

While I was working behind the scenes to support teachers, my wife was on the front lines, grappling with the emotional well-being of her students. She was growing increasingly concerned as she witnessed the emotional toll two months of the pandemic had taken on her students. She did her utmost to transform this period of continuity of learning into a positive experience, but the stress of providing online instructional resources was palpable. It was gradually eroding our spirits. Despite our efforts to persevere, we felt our energy, happiness, and motivation being drained away.

Consider the perspective of a young child living in an uncertain world, surrounded by constantly stressed adults. It's an uncomfortable environment. Even being around a single stressed individual can be anxiety-inducing, but during the pandemic, stress seemed to infect the entire world. The ongoing pandemic continued to weigh heavily on our children, our families, and our lives.

My fourth grader, who should have been forming small peer groups and close friendships, was suddenly cut off from her peers. She should have been learning about cooperative play and sportsmanship but found herself isolated from her friends. Instead of developing her own identity and beginning to separate from her family, she was practicing social distancing.

Meanwhile, my sixth grader, who should have been nurturing empathy for others and honing leadership skills, had to grapple with the loss of her peer communities. As she was experiencing the changes in her body, she had only her parents to turn to for guidance. This was supposed to be the time when she began processing more complex emotions like fear, frustration, rejection, and loneliness, but the closure of schools left her socially isolated.

My fourth grader resorted to writing letters and scheduling visits to maintain some connection with her friends. In contrast, my sixth grader, who was playing ice hockey, had to take a break when everything shut down. However, as soon as the rinks reopened, she eagerly returned to the sport, immersing herself in the camaraderie and challenges it offered.

Luna became our answer to these challenges. We were teaching our daughters to embrace our new pet weeks before she arrived. They were to be an essential part of the pack, always above the dog. They needed to learn how to be leaders, how to train our pet, how to care for our pet, and how to form a bond with our pet.

We welcomed Luna into our family on June 2nd, and it felt like Christmas morning. In the weeks leading up to this special day, we eagerly prepared for her arrival by collecting various dog supplies like toys, leashes, clickers, brushes, poop bags, and cozy beds. Our shopping list was inspired by the advice and recommendations we had seen on shows and YouTube videos dedicated to dog care. Additionally, we maintained constant communication with the breeder to ensure everything was in order.

Since we were the fourth family to respond, we had the privilege of choosing the fourth pick of the litter, almost like participating in the NFL draft. We watched videos of the puppies and received detailed scouting reports from the breeder. Our primary goal was to determine the perfect personality traits for our new furry family member. We debated whether Luna should be active, excited, smart, large, or small, considering every possible characteristic.

The litter of puppies was named after sprouts, with three of them being blond and the rest black, some of which had charming white spots and patches. Lavender captured our hearts with her boundless energy and curiosity. The big day finally arrived, and we embarked on an hour-long journey to pick her up from the breeder. The breeder was exceptionally thoughtful, providing us with a goodie bag and a stuffed animal that carried the comforting scent of Lavender's litter. Lavender became an official member of our family, and we later renamed her Luna.

We knew the dog was not the same as peers, but there are a lot of similarities. Training takes time, thought, and effort. Even our best efforts fail sometimes. Communication is key, just like talking to friends. Empathy and trying to figure out how to meet the pet's needs is a critical skill that must be developed by pet owners. Maintaining your standing in the pack is just like maintaining your standing in your friend group, you need to understand the messages your actions are sending and how they affect the group. Luna was a good substitute for the experiences our daughters were missing, but a pet cannot replicate everything a friend teaches us. A pet is only one individual; our daughters missed out on small and large group interactions and skills.

Chapter 3
Virtual Learning
(Fall 2020-February 2021)
or the
Social Media Substitute

I am old; I have been in school my whole life, either learning or teaching or both. I have some vivid memories of certain substitute teachers. Growing up, the substitute was an early birthday present, a surprise, a newfound treasure. I never really thought about it much since we didn't have them all that often. But I remember several. Not because they were awesome, but because they were horrible, and we took advantage of them. I still feel guilty about how they were treated.

In eighth grade, we had a business class, and the teacher was mean. He would lose his temper, scream, yell, and throw desks. Really, I saw him throw a desk in anger. Truth be told, I have had a couple of classes that made me want to act this way. Fortunately for me, I was able to collect myself and regroup instead of indulging my impulses.

On day, we showed up to this teacher's class and a substitute was sitting behind his desk. It was a weird moment; we didn't cheer, but we all looked at each other and just smiled. The year was 1986 and society was very different. zaps were our version of the spinner fidget toy, and everyone wanted to play.

A zap is a piece of paper folded over and over to become thick. Then it was bent in the middle. If you had a rubber band, you could use it to launch the zap across the class at a high velocity. It was quick, easy to conceal, easy to make, and it hurt. The hallways were battlegrounds, and everyone was a target. We were all trying our best to make the best zap, to get the best rubber band, to get the heaviest paper. The arms race was on.

Unfortunately for this substitute, she showed up in the middle of this arms race to cover a class for a teacher we all hated. We had to watch a movie. Old school, reel to reel movie. The Substitute was a mess. She had no idea how to set up the projector, lacked classroom management skills, and had no confidence. We could smell the fear, we could feel the weakness. We tested her like a predator testing prey. It was a work of art. It was horrible, but the way we all came together to take advantage of this teacher was impressive.

It started with one zap when the lights were turned off. We all heard it hit the wall. We reacted by getting lower in our seats and scouting the class for a guilty look. The teacher jumped at the sound and reacted poorly. She said something, I cannot remember what it was, but it was not the reaction the class expected. The combination of the jump scare and the poor reaction was the green light we needed.

You could hear people opening notebooks and tearing paper. You could feel the evil grins on your back and hear uneasy giggles. Everyone was a target. It started like a slow rain. One zap here, one zap there. Again, the teacher was clueless; she didn't even get up from her chair to turn on the lights. As she continued to allow us to engage, the frequency increased. Eventually that classroom exploded into a storm of zaps.

That classroom became a battleground. We stayed in our seats, but we all partook in that epic battle. It was better than a food fight at lunch. The substitute actually hid under the desk. Then the movie ended, the lights came on, and we stopped. When the light came on, the floor was scattered with zaps. It reminded me of a New Year's Eve celebration, confetti everywhere.

I think about this class every now and then. I still cannot believe we did it. I cannot believe we treated her so badly. But she was not the only one we took advantage of; I remember one class when a friend of mine borrowed a girl's bottle of hairspray. He opened it up and poured some on the tile floor in the back of the science class. He lit the pool of hairspray on fire. That hairspray burned for almost 10 minutes and the substitute never knew.

The job of a substitute is hard. They are usually not trained, and they are usually young. They don't really get paid that much. They have to take over a class and try to follow lesson plans that they did not write. These lessons might cover topics that they have not thought about in years. They are temporary; here one moment, gone the next. I personally never worked as a substitute teacher because I thought it set you up for failure. It is a losing task. The students have no attachment to you and no reason to respect you. They smell weakness, and they take advantage of that weakness.

Now imagine if you had the ability to choose a substitute teacher whenever you wanted. We put students in front of a screen and said, "Learn," but we gave them access to a social media substitute. Not a real person for a period, but the constantly present internet. Any topic at their fingertips. Yes, we tried our best to lock the computers down, but cameras were off, multiple tabs were open, and they still had video games, TV, and their phones. We unintentionally gave our students access to a social media substitute for the entire length of virtual learning. Holy Moly!

Part 1 - Me and My Job

Throughout the summer, we devoted ourselves to training Luna, helping her adapt to her new name, establishing our pack dynamics, and exploring nearby parks, as well as venturing a bit farther. My lifelong love for adventure led us to enjoy local and not-so-local parks. The summer was filled with excitement and unforgettable moments.

As summer drew to a close, we embarked on a two-hour journey westward to visit my favorite state park and enjoy a white-water rafting experience with a group of families. It was an unusual time as the hotel was nearly empty, and restaurants only offered outdoor seating or placed us near large openings to ensure safety. Although we interacted with others, there was a lingering sense of caution and wariness about being around people.

With the start of the school year approaching, uncertainty loomed over us. The previous spring had been intense and stressful, but little did we know that even greater challenges lay ahead. The news and political climate were undergoing significant shifts, with people growing increasingly impatient and distrustful. Conflicting information from various sources only added to the confusion. The upcoming presidential election and the ongoing pandemic had become contentious topics, turning science into a subject of debate. Social distancing remained a requirement, masks became a point of contention, and the prospect of virtual schooling was set to continue until February 2021.

Virtual learning? It was a challenge faced by school districts across the country, and my district was no exception. Seeking input from the community seemed like a sensible approach, so the question arose: "What should school look like in August? Should we continue with virtual learning, or should students have two days of in-person instruction per week and three days of virtual learning?" However, seeking community input opened a Pandora's box of opinions and conflicting desires.

Parents were eager to see their children back in school, but teachers and doctors voiced concerns about the safety of such a move. In a world that had embraced the idea of working from home, we grappled with the notion of putting our kids at risk. The prospect of virtual teaching was daunting for everyone, as it raised questions about how working parents would manage their children at home. Logic often seemed to take a back seat as parents passionately defended their viewpoints. Unfortunately, our children were not shielded from this heated debate.

The tide began to turn, with parents directing their frustration towards the school system. Families painted teachers and the education system as selfish and lazy, which was far from the truth. All of this was heard by our children. Ultimately, after being bombarded with a plethora of opinions, our system decided to continue with virtual learning. However, the damage was done.

Parents who had wanted their children to return to in-person learning grew even more frustrated, while teachers who were dedicated to providing the best education possible felt unfairly attacked. Our students were caught in the crossfire, forced to listen to frustrated parents blaming the school system. Morale was undoubtedly crushed, leaving everyone involved feeling disheartened.

When the fall of 2020 arrived, the rules governing education had changed once again. Instead of the expected continuity of instruction we had in the spring, we found ourselves navigating the world of online learning, with tools like Google Meets and direct virtual instruction becoming the new norm. Classes were a mix of synchronous and asynchronous learning, resulting in increased screen time for all students. Class schedules were inching closer to their pre-pandemic format.

In our district, middle school students experienced a blend of two days of direct instruction, two days of asynchronous instruction, and a fifth day designated for teacher office hours, enabling students to check in with each classroom teacher and address their individual needs. On average, students had direct instruction for each class on either Monday and Thursday or Tuesday and Friday, with Wednesday reserved for office hours and the other two days for asynchronous work.

Over the summer, my district made a concerted effort to select quality apps and programs that prioritized the safety of our students. They entered the new school year with a well-thought-out plan, a list of approved programs for use, and a platform for both students and teachers to work from. They were as prepared as they could have been, given the circumstances.

Personally, I was determined to embrace the challenges of this new reality. I work with a small, highly dedicated team, and I have the privilege of having an excellent boss, and his boss is excellent as well. Our unique position does not involve grading students, but we do teach every 5th and 6th grader in our school district.

Prior to COVID-19, each student would spend two full days with us. The four of us would pick them up from their regular schools when the morning bell rang, and we'd embark on a day of exploration in our county. We would return the students to school five minutes before the final bell. The first day, we would explore the south part of the county, and the second day, we would explore the north part of the county.

We taught fifth graders about geology and local history, and we taught sixth graders about ecosystems, watersheds, and biodiversity. Teaching outdoor school is a dream job; have I mentioned that yet? It was all the best parts of teaching. It was immersive, hands-on instruction and learning. Every day, several students would say, "This is the greatest day of school ever!"

Teaching outdoor school online, however, was far from enjoyable. I humorously referred to it as "indoor/outdoor school." In the previous spring, we had to condense our lessons into Google Slideshows, videos, Pear Deck lessons, and interactive activities. We had over three days' worth of instruction to divide into manageable, stand-alone lessons. Our goal in the spring of 2020 was to create teacher-ready resources for all our educational materials. In the fall of 2020, we changed our goal to take over teaching for the classroom teacher for a week.

Despite the challenges, my boss and his supervisor were unwavering in their commitment to keep our program alive. In a time when the world was in crisis, my boss's supervisor placed immense trust in our team to develop high-quality resources to assist teachers. She allowed us the autonomy to do what we believed was necessary to support educators during this challenging period.

My boss is undeniably an exceptional teacher, and his unwavering focus centers on safeguarding our program, which he considers his own. He took on the role of its guardian when he assumed his position, and every decision he makes is guided by a fundamental question: "Is this the best choice for our program?" While this might appear straightforward, it involves a multitude of variables, with considerations for student access, engagement, and exposure at the forefront. Over the past twelve years, he has continually challenged us to elevate our program to its highest potential. We've experimented, adapted, and refined our approach, and I take immense pride in the depth of content we cover and the high level of instruction we provide.

In the fall of 2020, my boss had a well-thought-out plan from the start. Our team embarked on the task of transforming our sixth-grade program into a three-week unit that we could share with fellow teachers. We meticulously crafted a week of pre-trip instruction, catering to both synchronous and asynchronous learning days. Additionally, we designed a week for direct student engagement with accompanying asynchronous work and a follow-up week of lessons. The ultimate goal was to make this resource available to every middle school within our district and to have us teach the week of direct instruction.

Teaching online posed an entirely new set of challenges, much like continuity of instruction did the year before. Factors such as access and signal strength, the number of people using the internet at home during Google Meet sessions, workspace limitations, attendance tracking, and camera usage became major obstacles. Our system embraced Google Meet as online meetings became the norm. Teachers gained the ability to share screens, mute students, and monitor chat rooms, but this also brought its own set of challenges.

One significant change was the window into our students' homes, which was both a blessing and a curse. We heard younger siblings in the background, glimpsed parents in the household, and quickly decided we couldn't mandate students to keep their microphones and video cameras on. It became overwhelming as we adapted on the fly. Although we had initial expectations as teachers, they were shattered for most of us in the first week.

To be clear, we did have ideas and expectations that we tried to implement initially. However, it soon became evident that peering into some students' homes was more of a distraction than an advantage. Listening to the background noise in some students' households added unnecessary stress. As a result, our system had to recalibrate its expectations. Cameras became optional, microphones were muted, and the chat box was disabled. After these adjustments, we grappled with student engagement.

One of the strengths of my team is that we teach the same lessons, allowing us to continuously refine and improve our content. Most of my colleagues discovered effective ways to engage our students and actively shared successful strategies with one another. Having coworkers to talk to and exchange ideas with was such a powerful resource.

During this time, I often thought of my wife, who was also navigating the challenges of online teaching, albeit without a team of coworkers for collaboration. She did have some lesson ideas that our district leadership team worked on over the summer, but a general lesson is not the same as a lesson you craft. She was constantly frustrated with the quality of the lessons they produced. It took her longer to adapt the canned lesson than it did to make her own. She was tired and stressed. While my wife and I shared and discussed our experiences, it was not the same as having a dedicated team to collaborate with. I was constantly grateful for the exchange of ideas that I had with my teammates.

My team used an app that allowed us to assign individual Google Slideshows to each student, which they could edit. They had the freedom to match, select, and draw, and as the teacher, I could monitor each student's progress and view their results. We had the capability to embed videos, although not YouTube videos, as our school district's policy did not permit it. Consequently, we had to create our own WeVideos. I put in extensive effort, constantly revising and refining those lessons. Furthermore, we continued collaborating with teachers in Google Meets while taking instruction in their classes, all while dealing with the aforementioned challenges of virtual teaching.

I am passionate about teaching, about witnessing that moment when my students grasp a concept, and about nurturing their creativity and curiosity. However, teaching through Google Meets was a far cry from the in-person teaching experience I cherished. It felt like I was teaching "Skittles," with each student confined to a small window displaying a circle containing the first letter of their first name. The circles had different colors randomly assigned. My students' faces were replaced with a circular icon that reminded me of the candy pieces found in a pack of Skittles. I could no longer see them grasp a concept. I didn't even know if they were in the meeting. They could have signed on and gone to the kitchen to eat. I had little to no feedback. One of the biggest shocks was the quiet. I remember teaching the first lesson and hearing nothing. Just me talking. It was so unsettling. I never realized how much the background noise helps me read my students and adapt my lessons.

The early days of Google Meets were plagued with numerous glitches, including frozen screens and microphone feedback. Cameras were quickly turned off, students were muted, and nonverbal communication was severely limited. As a teacher, I struggled to assess my students, and the teaching methods I had relied on throughout my career were no longer available to me. I found myself increasingly stressed, and a sense of depression and exhaustion began to overwhelm me. I no longer enjoyed going to my classroom. I no longer looked forward to teaching. I felt like a failure. Without the ability to see my students, I was just talking. I constantly felt like my students were not learning, not excited, and not engaged. I became obsolete, and it crushed my spirit.

I was constantly asking myself, my wife, and my coworkers about their lessons. I worked and reworked my lessons. Eventually, my hard work did pay off. A small win here and other victories there, plus the wins that my wife and coworkers shared. We were figuring out the riddle that was virtual teaching. There was hope! I was occasionally reminded why I loved teaching in the first place.

One of my most significant successes came in my salamander lesson. I created a slide that asked students to label the parts of a salamander, connecting words with the various body parts like legs, head, tail, and eyes. I challenged them to use color and then invited them to draw their own salamander on the next slide. This seemingly simple activity transformed my teaching. Students became fully engaged with the task, and I could display real-time examples of their work, offering compliments and adding countdown timers to maintain a sense of structure. The task became real, visible to peers, and each student adhered to the same time limits. My students embraced this format and the opportunity to showcase their abilities.

They became excited, and while I hadn't created a playground, I had established a shared sandbox where we could all build something similar. It was a concept both simple and powerful. As I shared their drawings, the colorful "Skittles" disappeared, revealing their faces for a few seconds. Microphones came to life, and we heard quick voices say things like "That's mine" and "Can you show my pic?" Virtual light bulbs seemed to illuminate as excitement permeated the virtual classroom. This engagement even reeled back in students who had momentarily lost focus, with some requesting to reset the timer so they could try again. The lesson was truly engaging.

Another major turning point occurred on October 7th, 2020, when my boss introduced a groundbreaking teaching approach that revitalized my passion for teaching. He decided to livestream a lesson, with one teacher managing the Google Meet, my boss in the field, and two of us monitoring the virtual classroom. He transformed the lesson into a "choose your own adventure" experience, allowing students to use the chat box to ask questions and direct the teacher as he explored a small creek watershed.

I watched him teach two lessons consecutively and then eagerly jumped in my car and joined him in the field. We found our playground! This innovative approach revitalized our lessons for the remainder of the year, rekindling my excitement and sense of purpose. It felt like genuine teaching, and our students were captivated. This transformative moment saved me. It was the playground all over again. We got to set the rules, we got to explore the challenges together. There was real-time excitement, feedback, and questions. Our learning community was dynamic and exciting. We found our fun!

Part 2 - The Changes and Challenges Students Faced

Despite our school system's establishment of a virtual learning environment and use of a standardized platform for organizing and communicating with students and families, students faced a significant learning curve in navigating this digital landscape. Additionally, we implemented direct instruction, requiring students to be present at specific class times. Although we distributed hotspots and Chromebooks, reliable high-speed internet remained a necessity for many.

Our initial expectation that students keep their cameras on during class quickly proved impractical as students felt uncomfortable exposing their living spaces. This expectation was swiftly abandoned. We also aimed to engage students by asking questions and encouraging discussion via microphones. What we heard through the microphones was often surprising, leading us to switch to the chat box for feedback. The initial weeks were challenging, as we all grappled with making the best of a difficult situation, and most students followed along.

However, some students continued to struggle with unreliable internet access, including my niece, who ultimately shifted to homeschooling because our system didn't meet her needs. Other families faced issues with multiple Chromebooks running simultaneously, causing terrible feedback when microphones were on. As a result, earbuds, headphones, and muted microphones became the new norm. Imagine being in a class but not being able to see or interact with the other students. That simple look across the classroom when someone says something silly and that shared smile or eye contact was gone. All of those "me too" moments were erased. We were alone on our computer.

For our students, the rules had changed yet again. School became more intense, with a standard class load featuring both synchronous and asynchronous lessons, deadlines, and grades. Cameras and microphones were predominantly turned off, and students had to adapt to a new system for classes, grades, and teacher communication. Missing assignments resulted in a 50% grade. The zero was eliminated. But we were back to teaching. Parents struggled to keep up, while most students quickly acclimated to the new normal.

A shift was occurring among our students; they were becoming masters of this new virtual school environment. They navigated the ever-changing rules and quickly adapted to the evolving landscape. It was a monumental task for parents to keep up with their child's work and progress.

This role reversal was significant between parent and child. At a time when students were seeking independence, they were handed the reins. Instead of relying on us, they made their own rules and lived by them for months.

They quickly discovered they could have multiple tabs open. While they were in lessons they could also be on social media. Some students would log into classes and then switch to playing games in another tab. Others would check in and then turn off their cameras and leave the computer altogether. Frustration grew, both for students and educators. Our school system tried to lockdown YouTube and other social media sites, but the students were always three or four steps ahead.

Remember walking down the hall and wishing you had a substitute teacher? When you saw a new person in the school the rumor mill would kick into high gear and hope sprung. "I hope it is my class that has the substitute teacher." During virtual learning, students could choose to have a substitute teacher every class: just open a new tab. I know that finding a good substitute teacher is hard. As a student, I had substitute teachers that I treated poorly, and it fills me with guilt. As a teacher, I now know the value of the material and the importance of the order in which it is presented and the connections that are made.

A substitute teacher is like a babysitter. A parent understands the value of the routine, diet, and expectations. A babysitter does not unless they are super responsible or long term. Similarly, a substitute does not understand the class routines or values unless they are passionate about the material they are overseeing. I have had some babysitters that were not good, and I have had lots of substitutes that were not good. How could they be? They are trying to get a paycheck; meanwhile parents and teachers are trying to achieve a valued goal, sometimes several. I am accountable for the class, and I am accountable for my daughters. I have a huge interest in the results, and no one can live up to my expectations.

We unknowingly gave our students the ability to have a social media substitute. Holy S@#%! Do we really want our kids to learn how to act from social media? Do we really trust social media to teach our kids values or raise our kids responsibly? We need to fire the social media substitute immediately.

We also need more patience. During the upheaval caused by Covid, our patience dwindled. We all yearned for the pandemic to end, yet our country found itself embroiled in arguments about the best course of action. Misinformation, disinformation, lies, half-truths, and frustration permeated our discourse, and our children were not immune to it. Trust in the news, our leaders, and each other was eroding rapidly.

Trust is a powerful concept, the bedrock of any relationship, but it can be shattered in an instant, and it takes a lifetime to rebuild. Our leaders had damaged our trust. As our students grappled with online learning, they also had access to the internet and search engines, where they encountered conflicting information from their families. Trust had been lost, and information became open to interpretation.

Moreover, students attended classes only to see avatars or "Skittles" instead of their friends' faces. The simple act of seeing a friend's smile or frown was lost. Their voices were muted, and classmates were reduced to colored dots with initials. Imagine seeing a spot instead of your best friend, reading text instead of hearing your friends talk. This was the stark reality of what school had been reduced to for our children.

Part 3 - How My Family Reacted and Adapted

As a teacher, I was weighed down by stress and focused on my responsibilities. But as a parent, I was stressed and filled with worry. At home, my wife and I worked together to set up dedicated workspaces for everyone. Desks, computers, and headphones became essential school supplies, even for my wife and me. I remember scouring Facebook Marketplace in search of desks, adding a bit of excitement to the preparations for the first day of school. However, the list of school supplies looked vastly different from what we were accustomed to.

For the most part, my daughters adapted reasonably well to virtual learning. They did, however, miss their friends. Luckily, their teachers eventually organized Google Meets to allow students to hang out virtually. My oldest, at the time a seventh grader, seemed to thrive in this new environment. She once told me that traditional school was absurd, remarking, "Dad, I have to isolate Luna and remove all the distractions to teach her, but at school, my classroom is filled with distractions." Virtual learning suited her better. Meanwhile, my youngest daughter benefited from workgroups and group projects.

My wife and I were teaching online while the girls were attending their classes, and everything appeared to be fine on the surface. However, beneath the surface, the loneliness was real, and the virtual community paled in comparison to the vibrant school atmosphere. The uncertainty of the situation eroded hope, and it was challenging to balance our roles as teachers while tending to our own children. I could only imagine the complexity for families with more than two children; it must have felt like a full-time job.

Our youngest, at the time a fifth grader, was learning about fair play and sought out small groups for interaction. Game apps that allowed her to play with classmates filled her need for social connection. Any assignment involving group games consumed hours and hours of her time. Messenger apps became a lifeline to her friends, and she and her classmates used technology to create small peer groups.

Our oldest, in the midst of middle school, began staying after in Google Meets to hang out with her classmates. Breakout rooms became a popular feature, and our daughters found ways to meet their social and emotional needs virtually. They were building online communities to combat the isolation.

In my family, discussions revolved around masks, vaccines, mortality rates, Covid cases, and current events. We had family members trying alternative medicines based on what they read online, while extended family members argued about vaccines. The country had lost its way, and at a time when our children needed strong and reliable leadership, they were let down.

Picture being in a house that's on fire. Mom says to get out because it's burning down, while Dad insists you stay put because you're about 78% water by weight, and water can put out fires. Both pieces of advice hold some truth, but one parent's guidance is clearly better than the other. Emotions were running high, and our children had to process all of this while navigating the complexities of virtual learning.

Not to mention the unintended consequences of this argument. When the kid realizes that one of their parents' ideas is wrong and can even hurt them, their image of that parent collapses. I was devastated when I found out about my mom's extramarital affair. It seemed like her life as my mom was a lie. It crushed my brothers too. It took me years to come to terms with this betrayal. It was the beginning of the understanding that my parents are just people, they are not perfect, and I can't trust them to make the best decision for me anymore. Remember when you discovered that a friend was keeping information from you, or worse, lying to you, and you hated them for it? But now it is your parents or your leaders. Such a horrible situation to be in.

When my parents were going through their divorce and engaged in heated arguments, I distinctly recall my mom throwing dishes at my dad. This memory, even though it happened when I was just 8 years old, remains vivid in my mind. It deeply affected me, and now, at nearly 50 years old, I still carry that memory with me. It was a traumatic experience that left a lasting impact. I know where everyone was standing, and I can still hear the shrapnel hitting the walls around me.

Now, imagine parents engaging in fierce conflicts over topics like masks, vaccines, and the virus itself. How would such battles affect our children? My guess is that it would have a negative impact, one that would resonate for a long time. In some families, the Center for Disease Control became an object of contention, and what should have been advice turned into heated arguments.

Our children were caught in the crossfire, receiving mixed messages from authority figures and having to navigate the confusion. They witnessed a world where, if you disagreed with the rules, you could simply create your own. I don't believe this was intentional, but it was the prevailing model everywhere you looked. We regressed to playground rules, where the loudest voice was considered right, where the last person to speak was right, and where the most persuasive speaker was right. We seemed to have lost our collective sanity, our hope, and we desperately tried to impose our will on each other without fully considering the effects on our kids. Ironically, we believed that everything we were doing was for their well-being, so they could return to a semblance of normalcy.

Gradually, we began to see more things opening back up. The ice rink, for example, was accessible, though you had to change outside and wear a mask. It wasn't ideal, but it was better than not being able to skate. My oldest daughter's ice hockey season began in September, offering her a group of friends to connect with. Meanwhile, my youngest scheduled visits with friends she could hang out with safely. We continued with dog training and hikes, even visiting a local ropes course. My main strategy was to stay busy so that we wouldn't have to dwell on the uncertainties surrounding us. In hindsight, it wasn't successful.

By October 8th, 2020, I was as emotionally drained as my kids, perhaps even more so. I felt utterly burnt out, and I recognized the urgent need for a break. I made the decision to take a week off, flying to New Mexico to meet up with my brother for some much-needed "mental floss," as Jimmy Buffett would say. I had to get away and focus on myself. This trip was pivotal in helping me regain my mental equilibrium. I am immensely grateful to have a loving and supportive family that allowed me to take this much-needed break.

During that week, I explored New Mexico and southern Colorado, finding solace and rejuvenation. I was able to jump in a car with my older brother and explore the world. I did not have to worry about anyone except me. My brother was the leader, and I was just riding his coattails. He had a plan and needed a copilot. Not having to be responsible for anyone else was glorious!

Upon my return from New Mexico, the world seemed a bit brighter, and my teaching had transitioned to live streaming. This break allowed me to reengage with my family. Looking back, I wish we had all taken that break together as a family. I believe it would have been beneficial for each one of us.

By December, we felt like we were getting a handle on the situation. So, of course, our world changed again.

Chapter 4
Back to School- Hybrid Learning

My team's transition to streaming lessons in October was a dynamic and exhilarating learning curve. As we found our rhythm, my team would shift from being outdoors one day to conducting Google Meet sessions the next. We established a rotation and began to gauge what resonated most with our students. In our roles as on-site instructors, we led lessons through creeks and fields, educating students about watersheds while they followed us from home. Traditional teaching tools were replaced with headsets, hotspots, tripods, and smartphones.

This teaching model truly revitalized me. It allowed us to bring students outside and immerse them in our world. I often felt like I was hosting a show on the Discovery Channel or National Geographic, but with a crucial difference – I could interact with my students. Our explorations transformed into real-time "choose your own adventure" experiences. Questions like "Which way should I go? Stream or trail?" were posed, and my students could answer these questions and direct our class. It was a genuinely exciting and unique experience.

Being outside, navigating through creeks, and discovering live critters to showcase to my students was immensely rewarding. It was undoubtedly challenging but also incredibly enjoyable, engaging, physically demanding, and dynamic. In essence, we had turned the lemons of our situation into high-quality lemonade.

We honed our techniques and developed our roles. The meeting monitor would talk to the home teacher and monitor the lesson, jumping the screen from teacher to teacher and watching the monitors for students' questions and concerns. We would troubleshoot problems and monitor the time. We would also watch the chat box and mute students that got too excited.

Our only limitations in the field were our willingness to move and time. I was able to find things that I loved and share them in my lesson. It was great. I could also chime in on my teammates' lessons. This interaction helped keep the students engaged and tied in the sections. We could foreshadow the topics that were coming up next or review topics we just talked about. We found our groove and it was really cool. Not as cool as having the students with us, but close. However, more chaos was to come.

Part 1 - Me and My Job

November marked the presidential election, and December brought the beginning of COVID-19 vaccinations. Meanwhile, my school district decided to initiate hybrid learning, just as we were starting to figure out how to make distance learning work. The educational landscape was shifting once more, driven by state mandates and preparing us for hybrid/concurrent teaching. The plan was for teachers to return to school on January 13th, 2021, to set up and get ready, with students scheduled to start on January 28th.

On January 6th, the teachers got some bad news and some worse news. The bad news was that the return to school would be delayed due to a spike in COVID-19 cases. Maybe this was good news. The worse news was that the Capitol building faced an attack. The significant day seemed almost too surreal to acknowledge. Teachers received two critical announcements on that day, one offering guidance on how to discuss the attack with our students and the other breaking the news that hybrid learning would be postponed until February 16th.

From a teaching perspective, the delay in returning to school did give us more time to process and prepare for our students. However, I know it was disappointing for a lot of people. Expectations can bring forth a mix of emotions, including stress, anxiety, and excitement. It's akin to waiting in line for a roller coaster, watching it repeatedly as your heart races with anticipation. You finally take your seat, buckle up, and the moment is about to arrive. However, instead of the ride beginning, your seat is unlocked, and you're told to disembark.

This is likely what our teachers and students felt during the constant delays in reopening schools and returning to normalcy. Some may have chosen to get back in line, while others may have decided to wait before embarking on this ride again. Regardless of their choices, it undoubtedly had an impact, perhaps inducing disappointment or heightened fear. Such stress takes its toll. It stressed my wife out.

As students returned to school, the rules and expectations were changing yet again. Those who opted for in-person learning had two days of in-person instruction each week, either Monday and Tuesday or Thursday and Friday, with the remainder of the week being virtual. To meet the state's new mandates, concurrent learning became a necessity. This meant that teachers had to instruct the students in the classroom while simultaneously running a Google Meet session for students at home.

The returning students had to adapt to new expectations, including mask-wearing, social distancing, hand sanitizing, increased personal hygiene, and interacting with students online. It was a complex situation that quickly became challenging to manage. Monitoring a classroom under normal circumstances is intense, but now add another layer: a smart board with remote students using text boxes and cameras.

In the classroom every piece of technology is a chance for something to go wrong. Microphones will give feedback if two are one in the same room. So now everyone had to have headphones in the classroom if more than one screen was being used. If teachers had old technology, everyone was on a screen. If a teacher had new technology, they could project a google meet on one screen and have one microphone going. But the teachers had to teach and monitor everyone, their screens, and every screen at home. The task was simply impossible.

They also had to manage the cohorts, Monday-Tuesday, Thursday-Friday, and the total virtual students. Everything had to be equitable, every student needed to have equal access. The demand took time. The teachers were exhausted. It was a colossal challenge.

Balancing all these elements as a single teacher was incredibly demanding. Nevertheless, my district managed it, and my wife successfully navigated this new teaching model as well. However, she started to change her attitude towards the powers to be. She was getting angry. A lot of teachers were angry. Just when the teachers were getting comfortable with the situation, our leadership changed the rules and expectations. Most of these changes seemed to be implemented due to public pressure, not science or data, and my wife felt like she did not matter to our leaders. She felt undervalued and underappreciated, which made her angry since she was working her butt off to make sure that her students were getting the best education possible in these horrible circumstances.

My team continued to stream our classes live on Google Meets, but we closely observed concurrent teaching and were continually impressed. There were multiple advantages to teachers being in the same room as their students. It allowed for the building of stronger relationships, informal assessments through body language and eye contact, support for students' emotional well-being, and immediate individual feedback. These changes were undoubtedly positive, but they also came at a cost.

Spending three and a half hours daily in a room with people while watching COVID-19 cases rise was anxiety-inducing. We heard reports of people contracting COVID-19 but not self-reporting, which raised concerns. Teachers were going to work in fear. The knowledge that they could potentially get sick and bring the disease into their homes was a terrifying thought. It was an incredibly challenging time to be a teacher. Especially since we were working around kids, who infamously do not take hygiene as seriously as adults. It was difficult to teach without imagining the germs on every surface, worrying that we would bring them home to our loved ones. I think every teacher had a kid that never changed their mask. Not only could you see the dirt on the mask, but you could also smell the sour odor when you walked by. Urging the kid to take a new mask could feel futile since they sometimes refused, claiming they trusted their mask more.

Simple tasks became complex. Social distancing, previously emphasized as six feet, became challenging to measure effectively. The guidelines, which we had followed for nearly 11 months, began to feel more like suggestions than rules. For instance, placing a dot at the center of a desk and drawing a six-foot circle around it was how social distancing guidelines were met in the classroom. But everyone can see that a student is larger than a dot. As a teacher responsible for students, this felt disheartening. As a teacher with high-risk category parents, it was truly terrifying.

Perhaps the most challenging aspect was dealing with the reactions of friends and family. Many of them were eager to see students return to school and seemed to have little empathy for our needs and emotional well-being. They wanted what was best for the students, and if teachers didn't like it, they suggested finding another profession.

The sentiment seemed to be that essential workers had been at work the whole time, so teachers should stop complaining. Comparisons to essential workers like Walmart clerks or construction workers didn't account for the unique challenges we faced in the education system. The clerks had plexiglass shields and only had to be around their customers for minutes at the most. Construction workers were mostly outside with the same crew. We were in a small room with our students for hours, no plexiglass.

It was discouraging, and we became the targets of frustrations from those who simply wanted the best for their children. But teachers don't determine how the school system works; we are merely employees. We have to do what the state and local school boards decide. Screaming at me, belittling me, and making me the target of your frustration will do nothing to affect policy. Some members of my family wanted to argue that teachers were a bunch of whiny little kids, and we should stop complaining about our working conditions. The whole time I was being yelled at, I was wondering when I brought this topic up. I realized later that I was asked what I thought, and I said it didn't make sense to me, that the data did not match their cutoffs. That opened the floodgates, and I was the target. At a time when everything was stressful, teachers became targets.

Teachers had already endured seven months of personal challenges, starting before the school year began. They had to create and implement systems on the fly, and now they were transitioning once more to concurrent teaching. Their resilience and dedication were remarkable, given the immense stress we all felt. I personally hit a breaking point in October. If being thrown into the deep end in the fall felt overwhelming, this new situation felt like being lost at sea. It was inevitable that important details might be overlooked. The small details, the things people take for granted. The lunchroom, the bathroom, the hallway, clean up, and dismissal. So many details, so many expectations, so many skills.

My wife went back into the classroom with mixed emotions. She is a math teacher at heart and there is always a right answer. She is also very efficient. When someone does not pay attention to details it drives her crazy. For her, "a couple" is always two and "a few" is three or more. So, when the school opening was delayed, she felt relieved.

When she went back to school, she was excited to see her students, and she was really upset with the students that did not follow the rules. We had guidelines for future school closures, but they kept changing. Case numbers in schools, classrooms, and our school system were being reported, but not in real time. Parents and Facebook always knew of students that had Covid, and the dashboards did not show those cases. When the community cases surpassed the health department's threshold for initiating a partial shutdown, the health department would just raise the required number of cases. It was becoming increasingly clear that schools would not shut down on a large scale again. Teachers were anxious, tired and tense.

Part 2 - The Changes and Challenges Students Faced

While the vast majority of students returned to virtual school, some did not. Our school system does not have reliable internet everywhere. We have populations of students that cannot afford the internet. Elementary school kids that cannot read or type had a real challenge getting online and doing work. This was a system that worked for most students, but not all. Students with accommodations were not getting them in a timely manner; it was tough. It was impossible to be equitable, but our system tried its best.

This was the driving force in getting the students back into the classroom. We cannot meet their needs when they are at home, so let's get them back in the buildings. The conditions and parameters set by the health department were the defining data points. They did not change fast enough for some families.

The decision to return to school or not was a pressing question for families and students alike. On November 11th, my school board voted in favor of the hybrid model for the second semester which started in January. Additionally, the Return to Play committee's recommendations were accepted, leading to the commencement of modified sports seasons on December 7th for winter sports.

As the vaccine development progressed, the FDA granted emergency authorization for the vaccine in December, with the first public shot administered on December 14th primarily targeting older adults. Children aged 12-15 would have to wait until May for the vaccine to be approved for them. In our state, teachers were placed on the priority list. Consequently, families and students found themselves pondering whether they should return to school in January.

Students did get a small victory with the return of sports. This is such a powerful community to be a part of. In high school, I loved being part of the football team, wrestling team, and track team. I loved being in the school play. These activities were so important to me that I joined teams and clubs in college and coached teams when I became a teacher.

Students got to rejoin a community they lost, and they got to search for the hidden synergy. I did not witness this; I teach middle school. But I recall hearing stories from friends about how important this was to their children. Being a member of a sport often defines us, and students were finally getting this back. However, getting the sport back and knowing all the rules, etiquette and expectations are different things.

When they opened the locker rooms at the ice rink, we had major issues with our athletes. They did not know how to treat each other. They did not know how to talk to each other. Their actions resembled social media. They wanted likes and reactions and did not understand that the consequences could be negative. The social media substitute retaught my athletes the rules, and I did not think about it until I was forced to react to it. It was so bad we had to remove locker room privileges for athletes and put parents in the locker rooms. Again, I wish I was in a place to really think about why this was happening, but it has taken time. I am finally in a better spot, and I can finally reflect.

Returning to school meant adhering to a new set of rules and protocols. Students were required to wear masks, except when eating or drinking. Questions arose about the consequences of not wearing a mask, when to stay home, the return-to-school protocol after falling ill, the practicality of social distancing, and the necessity of COVID-19 testing. The guidelines were communicated to student families in early December. They had a deadline to make a choice. Come to school or stay virtual.

Then January 6th happened. For students who are battling anxiety, who are trying to find the truth through all of the fake news, this was hard. For students that are screaming for structure and stability this was hard. Students are curious, they want to know. We had to address our students' needs, and they asked questions. Tough topics like this are giant red flags for teachers, but natural magnets for students. Every teacher has to figure out how to deal with challenging subjects.

I was in the classroom when the 9-11 attacks happened. I had students whose parents worked at the pentagon. I had to deal with that in real time, and our students were confused and hurt. They wanted to call their parents, they wanted to go home, they wanted to start a war, they had crazy emotions and reactions, just like the rest of us. My classroom was a safe place to vent and think. We talked about the attack; we addressed our fears so that we could move on the next day. Giving students time to process and explore situations helps prepare them for the next crazy event. It is the same with a fight in the hallway. You can try and keep your students from talking about it, but you will fight that battle the whole entire class period. I have found it is better to acknowledge the fight, let students talk about it and then move on.

Teachers had to deal with their students' curiosity and anxiety. Students had a safe place to ask questions, and teachers did their best to explain that our capital building was attacked, that the country was not at war, and that everything was going to be okay.

We had to try and make sense of a group of people, our people, attacking the symbol of our country. When we were trying our best to get our children's world back to normal, the symbol of our country was under siege. People were killed. The peaceful transfer of power was lost. We have been told our whole lives this is what distinguishes us from everyone else.

How does a student even process this? I have trouble processing this. The world is hard. The pandemic is hard. We are trying to get back to "normal," then this happens, and it is not normal. One more thing to add to our children's confusion. One more thing for our students to figure out. One more thing to divide our leaders, our parents, our respected adults. You have to wonder when the final straw will be added. You know, the one that breaks the camel's back. I am sure that for some of our children, that straw came long ago.

Students and families got to choose whether or not they would come back to school. I know that some were very excited, and some were not, but they were getting the chance to choose. I know some parents left the choice to their children; we were in that group of parents that did not.

My wife and I wanted to wait and see how it was going. We made the choice of keeping our daughters home. We knew they would have the chance to go back later. We really wanted to see if being in the classroom was going to work.

From the classrooms that I helped teach, I could see that students were benefiting from being back in a physical classroom environment. However, it was important to recognize that it was not the same as the pre-COVID classroom, nor should it have been. As adults, we understood this, but I'm not sure our students fully grasped it.

They might not have stopped to consider that the classroom environment was temporarily changing and would eventually shift back to something more familiar. We, as teachers, probably didn't explicitly teach this message because we ourselves were uncertain about what the future held. Unintentionally, we were reshaping the classroom environment with different expectations and rules, and our students were adapting to them. I believe my district did an excellent job, but everything was happening rapidly, leading to unintended consequences. These consequences affected everyone involved.

Teachers were breaking down, society was at its tipping point, and our school system kept asking everyone to do more. Children were learning to adapt to the changing classroom expectations. They were being taught to show up and keep away from each other. Some students were being taught to not report their illness. Some were learning that you showed up to class and got on a screen. Some were taught to communicate only in the chat bar so everyone could be included. Some were taught that the students at home were more important. I don't think this was intentional. I think these ideas were the unintended consequences of hybrid learning. Some were so overwhelmed they just shut down; teachers and students alike.

So often the boss asks for results but doesn't help you understand how to achieve them. Our school system is run by a board that has to answer to the state and the public. They wanted results but did not understand the details involved, such as the fact that not all schools have the same resources. The older schools and the elementary schools have less technology. It makes sense when you think about it. A new school has new money, and they can buy the newest supplies. An old school has to use part of its budget to get technology. It is phased in slowly and only if staff members demand it. And why put a kid in first grade in front of a computer? But now every classroom had to be able to run google meets while students were in the classroom so everyone had equal access. Even internet access is hard to get in some parts of our school system. The fine details that make things work well were missing in some schools. On top of that, everyone was exhausted.

Now, consider our students. They felt stress at home and in school, and it was only made worse by the things they heard about in the news. Their safe spaces and escapes had been eliminated. Despite all this, they seemed to be handling it remarkably well. Kids are resilient and survivors. From an outsider's perspective, they appeared to enjoy going back to school, at least for a little while. But our students and children are just like Shrek and onions; they have layers (*Shrek* 27:04-27:30). Of course they were happy to see their friends. Of course they were happy to go back to school. Of course it is exciting to be back at school. But being happy does not mean they were okay.

They lost skills, they lost opportunities, they lost confidence, they lost trust. Smiles are only the outside layer of the onion or ogre. The scars from this period of isolation and virtual teaching with social media substitutes are deep. I think it will be a long time before we truly understand the impact on our children.

As we transitioned into the hybrid model for the third term, in-person learning was a fresh start. My wife often discussed the initial frustration with the lack of attention to small details but found joy in reconnecting with her students. She could finally see her students, and she could see how excited they were to be back. Students at home tried, and at times succeeded, to reconnect with the students in the classroom. More cameras were on, and students could make eye contact with their peers in the classroom.

When the third term was coming to an end, the school system also allowed parents a second opportunity to choose whether they wanted to send their students to school. They had to inform the system by a certain deadline. As a result, the number of students attending school increased in the fourth term. It felt like a significant victory – returning to school, seeing friends, and leaving the confines of their homes. The case numbers were finally coming down and the vaccines were going to ready for 12-15-year-olds soon. The future was looking brighter.

Part 3 - How My Family Reacted and Adapted

Deciding whether or not to send our kids back to school was a challenging decision for our family. Our daughters were eager to return to school immediately, and we had many family discussions about it. Personally, it didn't initially make sense to me or my wife. Our primary babysitters are my wife's mom and stepdad. They are in high-risk groups and the last thing we wanted to do was be responsible for them getting sick. We had the ability to keep our kids home and see how the return worked, so we did.

Ultimately, we decided to keep them home for the third term, with the understanding that they could return in the fourth term if the numbers improved. They are still a bit upset with us for this choice. They knew the risks, we talked about our fears, but when they turned on the screen and saw their friends in the classroom, they were mad. They missed their friends so much they were willing to risk the safety of others that they loved. It reminds me of the marshmallow test. You sit a kid down and place a marshmallow in front of them. You give them a choice: they can eat the marshmallow right away, but if they wait 15 minutes, they will get two marshmallows. Our daughters were so hungry for social interactions with their peers they wanted to eat the marshmallow immediately. They missed their friends and all the things their friends provided.

Virtual learning seemed to be working for our family. Our daughters were finding success, and we had found our rhythm. We had adapted to life at home, and the idea of making a change was met with some resistance initially. Everyone was stressed; we were already experiencing so much change and unknown. To complicate matters further, my mother passed away during this time. She had been in a nursing home and had been unwell for an extended period.

Throughout the summer, my brothers and I would check on her and deliver groceries since she lived alone. In the fall, my sister-in-law found her stuck on the floor, and she was subsequently hospitalized and placed in a home.

Although we could visit her, it was far from ideal. Shortly after Christmas, she contracted COVID-19. Despite her fragile condition, she miraculously survived the virus, but she began to deteriorate slowly afterward.

My daughters were aware that she was unwell, but I had kept them somewhat isolated from her for years. My mother was an alcoholic. I used to visit her early in the morning, hoping we could get there before she was drunk. It only took one bad visit to understand that my daughters never needed to see her drunk ever again. I guarded my daughters from my mom, so they didn't have a strong attachment to her. I hope they remember the pleasant moments spent with her, like craft time and snacks on her porch, and that they forget the less pleasant ones.

When my mom was first hospitalized, she was only allowed one visitor a day. I tried to see her, I parked and tried to check in, but I was too late. She already had her daily visitor. I did go and see her when she was placed in a home. We talked about how she was unhappy; she hated everything. I was able to ask what she wanted and what she was looking forward to doing. We used this information to send care packages and I made phone calls. She got sicker, she moved to another hospital, she got better, she got the Covid vaccine, then she got Covid. Then she got better and returned to the nursing home. I was struggling emotionally.

It was especially painful for me to have my mom stuck in the hospital. Given my own history of asthma, I spent time in the hospital growing up. I remember the smells, the sounds, the pain and the unknown. The hospital was a prison to me. It was a place where my body failed, and dreams were replaced with pain and survival. The hospital is lonely. Everyone leaves you. Sure, they come to visit, but they will leave you alone with all the pain, all the noise, all the unpleasant smells. I wanted to see her but also didn't want to see her. However, when my little brother visited and reported that things were looking grim, I decided to go and see her on March 20th.

The facility that she was placed in made me suit up in hazmat gear, and I had a private visit with her in the hospital. I'm incredibly grateful for that hour. She recognized me and tried to speak, but she was too weak. I held her hand, comforted her, and said the things she needed to hear. She fell asleep, and I left. Sadly, the next morning, on March 21st, 2021, she passed away.

My family respected my need for space during this difficult time, understanding that losing a loved one is a profoundly painful and personal experience. Processing all of these emotions in the midst of a pandemic was overwhelming. Planning gatherings and speaking with relatives felt nearly impossible. In accordance with my mom's wishes, my brothers and I took her to the ocean and scattered her ashes in the salty brine, fulfilling her final request.

When I got back from the ocean, I was still an emotional mess. My mom was a hard topic to process. I had lost people before, but losing your mom is different. It is hard to explain; she has always been around. She was one of the few people I have known my whole life. She made me, and now she was gone. I am still trying to come to terms with this loss.

Once we put my mom to rest, I returned my focus to the family I had that was still alive. We were healthy, we were able to get online, we had jobs, I know I should have been happy, but I was not. Neither were my daughters.

My daughters couldn't help but feel jealous of their classmates throughout the entire third term. They could see their classrooms, knew where their friends were, and desperately wanted to be part of it all. The fear of missing out (FOMO) was almost tangible. Fortunately, their wish was granted in the fourth term when they were able to return to in-person hybrid learning.

Despite her excitement, my youngest daughter was a bit nervous about going back. She was part of the second wave, having to relearn the classroom expectations in front of the first group of returning students. Every cough was met with whispers of "COVID," and there was an unspoken unease in the air. Everyone kept their distance, lunch was mostly outdoors, and conversing with a friend from six feet away felt strange. She started to question what we were doing and why. The things being done in the classroom were not logical. Why do we have social distance at lunch when we are outside? Now we have to yell to talk to our friends. Isn't this worse?

My wife faced significant challenges with the hybrid learning model. Balancing the needs of both virtual and in-person learners was a complex task. Everyone had to be on Google Meet, with each student equipped with a computer and earbuds to hear their peers. Managing all of this as a single teacher was incredibly demanding, and it became clear that policymakers had little understanding of the immense stress they were placing on classroom teachers. Our family was just trying to hold it all together.

To provide ourselves with something to look forward to and pull us through the tough times, we decided to plan a big family vacation. My wife pushed for a family trip to Zion National Park. Zion is one of my favorites. Slot canyons, red rock and exposure. We first discovered Zion on our honeymoon. My wife and I hiked The Narrows from top to bottom. We hiked The Subway from the bottom up. We hiked Angels Landing. I wanted to share all this with our daughters, but this is difficult hiking. Ten miles a day, repelling, and walking in creeks.

Exploring this park meant embarking on challenging hikes with significant elevation changes. Zion is one of my favorite places in the United States, but to really access it you need to bring your "A" game. Considering our daughters' ages and my burning desire to explore the park to its fullest, we made a family commitment to get into hiking shape. This trip motivated us to work out twice a week and embark on weekend hikes to prepare for the adventure. It was a successful strategy leading up to the trip.

While this training did help mentally, the toxic stress had already accumulated; it was taking a physical toll on my body. My hip constantly hurt, which I attributed to long hours in front of a computer. It was likely a combination of stress, prolonged sitting, and inconsistent exercise. My left foot also started giving me trouble. My wife experienced frequent migraines and back pain. We were both falling apart under the weight of stress.

Our final hike before we left was a 10 mile out-and-back across the top of Old Rag, in Virginia. This is a monster hike. If you explore the granite peaks and climb over all the boulders it is very strenuous. So of course, that is what I made my family do. It was a full day and my family crushed it. They were in shape, they were excited, and they were prepared. No whining, no complaining, just enjoying the challenge. I was so pleased with my girls. They worked so hard; we moved with purpose to achieve this goal. I knew we were ready for Zion.

Our trip to Zion turned out to be an incredible escape for all of us. We pushed ourselves physically, hiking over twenty-three miles and climbing over 2,000 vertical feet in just three days. I couldn't have been prouder of my daughters and wife. We waded through The Narrows, tackled Angels Landing, and we navigated The Subway from top to bottom, only getting lost once. We did have a little help exiting the Subway. A monster thunderstorm chased us out of the canyon. The final climb out is hard. It is grueling. That storm was the kick in the pants we needed to focus and motivate our actions. Hearing the thunder echo off the canyon walls, as the sky turns black is awe-inspiring. It is also terrifying. Flash floods are public enemy number one to anyone in a slot canyon. Mother nature gave us the final push we needed to move up the canyon wall and get to the car. We accomplished my major goals. We completed our Varsity trip. The rest of the time was just icing on the cake.

To celebrate the completion of our last major hike, we enjoyed a victory dance: crepes. As part of the trip planning, we asked the girls to pick our restaurants for meals. They had found a little cafe that served breakfast crepes. We were exhausted, but my daughters found their second wind as they enjoyed celebratory crepes. My youngest indulged in mixed berry and cream cheese heaven while my oldest partook in cinnamon sugar yumminess. My wife got the chocolate and banana slathered sweetness, and I enjoyed a bacon cheeseburger. Looking around at my smiling family, I forgot about the sweat on our backs and the challenges of the pandemic.

The trip helped wash away some of the stress that had accumulated over the years. I felt rejuvenated, proud of my family, and ready to face the challenges of a new school year—or so I thought.

Chapter 5
Everyone is Back

Returning home from Zion, I was filled with excitement. The trip had been an absolute necessity for our family, offering the much-needed respite we all craved. With the end of summer, the realization dawned that school would soon be upon us. My oldest daughter was gearing up for ice hockey, and our youngest daughter was embarking on horseback riding lessons with a friend. Life was settling into a more tranquil rhythm, and our family was recharged.

As the school start date drew near, our school system made a pivotal decision to return to full-time, in-person instruction. It felt like a return to the pre-pandemic school routine, with one notable exception: everyone had to wear a mask. There was noticeable excitement in students and teachers alike. We felt as though we were finally leaving the challenges of the past behind and eagerly embracing the prospect of getting back to school, fully in-person.

Part 1 - Me and My Job

Starting the 2021-2022 school year, I can't recall feeling any fear. I had been vaccinated, as had my wife and oldest daughter. With the promise of vaccine approval for younger kids on the horizon, our school system was gearing up, ordering masks and hand sanitizer, and developing protocols for cleaning, social distancing, lunch, and addressing the learning gap. We knew this was going to be a significant change.

We returned to school on August 18th, 2021. From March 16th, 2020, to August 18th, 2021, our students had been grappling with major changes brought about by the pandemic. Over seventeen months had passed since they had experienced "normal" school. We could almost see the light at the end of the tunnel. I was happy, or at least, I believed I was. Looking back, "happy" may not be the right word; "optimistic" seems more fitting.

Our inboxes were flooded with emails about reigniting, reconnecting, and revolutionizing our students. The plan was to teach the whole student. We would focus on their mental health, physical health, social-emotional development, cognitive development, identity development, and close the achievement gap through academic development.

This might sound like a daunting task, and it is, but teachers do this every day, all day long. We notice when a student looks sad, when they're disengaged, or when they're struggling to learn. We pay attention to our students. Getting to know our students is an integral part of teaching. Creating a safe environment and providing resources so our students can feel comfortable enough to learn is what teaching is all about. Good teachers have always done this. It was heartening to see that those in charge recognized its value. As a teacher, I understood that all these elements needed to be in place to enable me to do my job effectively.

We also received guidance on fostering the right learning mindsets. We were encouraged to emphasize a growth mindset – the belief that we can all get smarter with effort. We were instructed to emphasize a mindset of belonging, where our students are an integral part of our community, and everyone collaborates effectively. Our emphasis was also on cultivating a mindset of purpose and relevance, ensuring that our students could discern a clear purpose in their tasks, thus motivating themselves to learn.

Furthermore, we were advised to guard against adopting a deficiency-oriented mindset, one that fixates on challenges and circumstances rather than recognizing potential. At times, it can become an excuse, almost enabling in nature. It is remarkably simple to observe a struggling student and attribute their difficulties to their circumstances, using this as a reason not to hold them accountable. For instance, assuming a student cannot work because they are hungry or cannot learn due to a lack of resources. Succumbing to this line of thinking can be perilous. Our central office consistently emphasized the need to steer clear of this mode of thinking. It is hard to learn when you are hungry, but that doesn't mean you cannot learn.

Teaching the whole child and fostering a growth mindset are integral components of great teaching. Reminding our staff about these key ideas is the sign of great leadership. However, it's essential to recognize that every message is received and processed differently by its recipients. What I failed to anticipate was how these concepts would be perceived by some of the administrators.

I also failed to realize that this school year would be the second most challenging of my life. Our students needed more support than I initially expected in order to return to a semblance of normalcy. It became evident how quickly the students forget. Constant changes in our structure and expectations had left our students bewildered.

What I overlooked was that my sixth graders had last attended in-class instruction when they were in the fourth grade, missing critical developmental and social milestones during the past year. Similarly, my fifth graders had been out of the classroom since their third-grade year, missing similar developmental and social experiences. My students were much like me—stressed, scared, navigating each day one step at a time, and unable to process the full extent of what had occurred and was still happening.

In my role as a bus driver taking kids on field trips, I recognized that our students hadn't been on a field trip in over seventeen months. My team understood the need for a gradual approach, allowing teachers to establish classroom routines and providing everyone with adequate time to adapt. Our primary focus was on the current sixth graders, aiming to offer them an experience as close to "normal" as possible—a two-day trip. Consequently, the fifth graders had to shorten their trip to one day. To help make up for this loss we developed a small fifth-grade lesson that could be done on the school campus.

Our plan was to visit all the fifth-grade classrooms between August 26th and September 24th, covering over 25 schools and teaching as many fifth graders as possible. We designed our lessons centered around exploring their school campus. Our approach was hands-on and engaging. We would introduce ourselves, get the students outside, and take them on a campus tour. This allowed the fifth graders to familiarize themselves with us and our teaching methods. We utilized various activities such as follow-the-leader, bingo scavenger hunts with stickers, and games like red light, green light, all while exploring important topics related to the earth's resources.

Students were genuinely enjoying their learning journey in their schoolyard, delving into the wonders of science. When we're passionate about something, we can't help but share our joy and enthusiasm. The students understood this, and the attitude became contagious. However, it wasn't without its challenges. The students had to wear masks inside the school building, which meant their whispers were barely audible, and reading lips was impossible. Encouraging students to speak up became quite a task.

Students seemed to forget basic classroom etiquette like raising their hands, and we noticed several small things were amiss. The classroom was quiet. Almost like the mask was a reminder not to talk. Students were nervous and unsure of their actions. These minor issues started to accumulate, and I was constantly contemplating how to enhance the situation. Improving communication, slowing down the pace, ensuring understanding, and revisiting expectations—all these strategies were essential, but I still encountered issues in nearly every class. I found myself needing to pause, redirect, and refocus much more frequently than before the pandemic.

Much like a classroom teacher, I had to assess classes on the fly, determining what worked, what didn't, and figuring out how to do it better the next time. It felt like a race, especially on days when we visited three schools. While I was having fun, I was also growing weary. Balancing our time with students while addressing disruptions and reteaching was a constant challenge.

However, there were several significant victories. We discovered that small games were effective, as was offering instant gratification through stickers. Encouraging students to share personal details about themselves also helped. While this might sound straightforward, we were working against the clock. Each class required introductions, explanation of expectations, transitioning outside, and tackling 3-4 major activities, all within a very short timeframe.

Then came September 15th, when we switched to working with sixth graders. It was a shock! In the past, we had always met these groups in the cafeteria, so we followed suit. We anticipated the need for organization, but what we encountered was a whirlwind of social interactions. Looking back, we should have seen this coming. For many of these students, it was their first time together in a large group setting in seventeen months. Everything took longer—everything.

To make matters more challenging, TikTok was promoting "back to school" challenges, some of which involved filming destructive behavior in school and posting it online. We hadn't expected the minor issues to become so overwhelming, but we should have anticipated it. We did not understand that the social media substitute was teaching our students while we were struggling with online learning. We did not understand that we had to unteach these behaviors. I am still battling the social media substitute in my current classrooms.

During our first six days at the middle school, we interacted with over 180 students. We conducted six trips, working alongside two of our favorite sixth-grade teachers, and we were genuinely taken aback. We encountered various disruptions, including a student posting a TikTok challenge video while in the bathroom, leading to administrative involvement and that student missing our trip. There were bathroom emergencies during instructions, students who refused to write things down, and groups of students leaving their designated areas without permission. While we were accustomed to dealing with these incidents throughout the school year, this was a continuous stream of minor emergencies that kept us on our toes. It was an intense experience.

When we conducted our first trip, the students had been back in school for nearly a month. Many of them still struggled to sit and listen attentively. Their classmates proved to be significant distractions, as they sought the attention of their peers. Focusing for extended periods was challenging, and a substantial portion of them lacked the persistence required to tackle difficult tasks. When faced with challenging situations, they often shut down. While this is not uncommon among students, it appeared to be more prevalent than before the pandemic. They also touched each other a lot, often hanging on each other.

I was genuinely shocked. We had chosen a school we held in high regard, with beloved teachers and a community known for its strong reputation, yet the students were having difficulty even in the cafeteria. The first day back, while watching the students in the cafeteria, my mind recalled a chaotic scene from an old cartoon, with blaring horns and sirens. I found myself in full-blown panic mode as I attempted to organize 30 students. I managed to figure things out, but those initial 30 seconds served as a significant wake-up call. I tried to elevate my voice to get their attention. I tried to wait for them to get quiet. None of this worked, so I walked to each group and asked them to explore our lab packet, pick a favorite page and be ready to explain why it is your favorite. Our lab packet is 16 pages. Every page is a different activity. This worked. They were focused, they wanted to share, and I was in charge. This was what I needed to gain control of my class.

As we moved from one school to another, we could predict the course of our day within the first 10 minutes based on how the students behaved in the cafeteria while receiving instructions. We knew which groups could refocus and which could not. We knew which students could work and follow directions and which could not. We take students outside. I want to explore everything with them, but I cannot take a group to the edge of a creek if they do not listen. I cannot joke with a group that cannot refocus. I cannot do all the fun, scary things with students I do not trust. Most schools required an additional 20-30 minutes in the cafeteria. It saddened me to realize that these children were missing out on really cool, valuable opportunities simply because they struggled to focus and listen. Their world had been turned upside down so many times that they didn't know which way was up. This loss was a huge struggle for me. I know how awesome my day can be, and I did not feel like my students were able to handle it. My soul hurt.

What many people may not fully grasp about teaching is that it only takes one student to disrupt an entire class. One student can shift everyone's focus, thereby stealing opportunities for learning. When there are two disruptive students, not only do they impede learning, but they also begin to challenge the teacher's authority in the classroom. If three students decide to rebel simultaneously, they can effectively take control of the class and create their own mini-community. When three students unite against the teacher, it becomes a herculean task to regain control and get the class back on track.

This is precisely the situation we were dealing with—small groups of students rebelling and doing as they pleased. They would stand up, walk around, leave the cafeteria, or even venture into other classrooms, creating a state of chaos. Fortunately, my team excels in classroom management, and we managed to address the chaos. Our initial shock eventually transformed into anticipation, as each of us developed our own methods for organizing the groups and capturing their attention. Exploring the packet and sharing students' thoughts and ideas were huge wins for me.

It took time. Sometimes teaching feels like a numbers game. Try this, and if it doesn't work, try this, and if that doesn't work, try this. I wish I could say I crushed it from the beginning, but I was trying to organize the chaos, and it took time to realize that students really wanted to share their stories. Exploring the packet got my students excited, asking them what they wanted to do most got them engaged. Asking them if they remembered us from virtual teaching helped out as well. But we were accessing their knowledge first. We were interested in them, and my students responded to this.

While no two schools were identical, they all exhibited similar patterns. During those initial two weeks, I felt mentally drained by the time we left the cafeteria and got on the bus to start the day. Luckily my classrooms are awesome, my students get excited, and this helps recharge my batteries. A visit by a bald eagle makes me smile all day long. Catching a snake and sharing it with my students is food for my soul. Many days I would feed off of my students' excitement, but I was drained at the end of the day. I constantly felt sorry for my wife and all the other teachers stuck in the school building.

We often had to manage anywhere from 60 to 110 students, and they only had two days with us. Every second we lost meant missing out on something valuable. In those early weeks, I couldn't help but feel disheartened. My primary goal was to provide students with the best day of school possible, but their behavior was hindering my ability to achieve that. Consequently, my approach evolved, and I began to explain to them that their behavior directly impacted their opportunities. I would stand in front of the bus with my arms stretched to my maximum wingspan and say, "I want to do this much stuff today!" Then I would say, "every time I have to repeat myself, every time I have to wait for you to listen, every time I have to ask you to focus, we miss out on things we get to do." As I was talking, I would bring my hands closer and closer together. This approach started to yield positive results, so I expanded my explanation. I would list the day's activities; I would talk about how they were choosing to hangout in the cafeteria instead of going on a turtle safari. This worked better for most groups, but not all. It took me longer to realize that some groups were scared of the trips. I loved trips, and still do, so this idea was not even on my radar.

We instantly became salesmen. We had approximately thirty seconds to ignite the students' excitement and get them to follow our directions for the next fifteen minutes so we could kick-start our day. If we faltered, we had to regroup and try again, sometimes repeatedly. It began to feel like I was Captain Hook, constantly aware of the tick-tock of the clock. I knew that we were missing out on some of the most enjoyable parts of the day, and I could see that some of my students were making choices they would come to regret. This feeling became an integral part of my sales pitch: "Today is your only day to experience this with us. Let's make the most of it." Of course, it was a lot more complex than that, and it took several trips to fine-tune my approach for the rest of the year.

Repeating a similar routine each day allowed me to experiment constantly, and I had both significant successes and one notable setback. Sometimes, it took a trip or two to fully grasp the significance of these wins. When I entered the fifth-grade classrooms in the beginning of the school year, I witnessed the tremendous power of small games. They were an instant hit, and student engagement soared. These games were exactly what they needed – an opportunity to interact with their peers, learn how to follow rules, and experience the joy of winning. The enthusiasm was so contagious that I found it difficult to bring the games to a halt. It was truly an awesome experience.

Another small win came from encouraging students to share something about themselves. For instance, I would share a humorous breakfast story to help fifth graders understand the term "conglomerate," which typically had about a 50/50 success rate when I just explained it directly. However, when I asked the class to share their favorite breakfast, engagement levels shot up to around 90-100%.

Recognizing the power of this approach, I started implementing it with other stories and ideas, and it consistently yielded impressive results.

Yet another small victory involved having students share their dreams. Simply asking them what they wanted to be when they grew up had a profound impact, helping me tailor my lessons to their interests. I could incorporate connections to their dream careers, making the learning experience more relevant and engaging. This approach turned out to be a major win for both the students and me.

My last significant victory took longer to develop. It began in the cafeteria while exploring our lab packet, continued on my bus as I addressed inappropriate behavior that was depriving other students of opportunities, and finally solidified when I started discussing the concepts of positive and negative attention. This distinction helped students understand whether the teacher was addressing them to curtail their behavior or because they wanted to encourage more of it.

However, these adjustments to my teaching style took months to fine-tune and, in the meantime, there were still obstacles. I distinctly recall one school where it took us over thirty minutes longer to get the students organized and ready to go. A handful of students consistently derailed the process to the point where we contemplated leaving them behind at school. In my twelve years of teaching outdoor school, out of roughly 39,000 students who have participated in our trips, I can count on one hand the number of times we've had to tell students they couldn't come. It's the absolute last decision we want to make, indicating just how challenging this situation was.

This group of students had no patience, no impulse control. They did what they wanted when they wanted to do it. They had learned this during virtual school. They were left at home to leave the computer to eat, drink, go to the bathroom or pick up their phone and chat with their friends. They were doing all of this. When they got bored or frustrated, they just stood up and went to talk to their friends.

When we inquired with the teacher about this group of students and whether they had discovered any helpful strategies, they responded that some things worked occasionally, but the students exhibited this behavior constantly. The teacher's responses were so basic that I don't even remember what she said. I was already working on newer and more complex approaches; I was so far past her suggestions that I became angry. I like to think that I have good classroom management; I am persistent, and I have grit. If I am asking for help, I need help. I don't need someone asking me if I've tried to talk to the students yet. Of course, I simply said I had already tried that, but my frustrations with the go-to methods of managing the kids were growing.

We asked if the teachers had received any support from the administration, and they explained that the administration did not impose any consequences on the students' actions. Instead, the administration told the teachers that they needed to get to know their students better. Talking to the administration was seen as a joke among students, and asking for help was seen as a joke among teachers.

I recognize that I made mistakes, and I understand that in hindsight, I could have handled things better. I'm not attempting to cast blame on anyone. I know our administrators were in a hard spot. But this administrator chose to use no consequences. I'm sharing this to help you understand the challenges our students were facing. We all need structure, and consequences provide that structure. When there are no consequences, the structure falls apart. The consequence also causes guilt. Students need the guilt to associate their actions with a bad feeling. It gives the student control by allowing them to notice patterns of "I did this, and I felt like this" or "it caused this." Realizing that their actions impacted themselves or their peers is what prevents the action in the future. This guilt helps children develop initiative. They start to understand they can control what happens.

I don't believe consequences need to be overly severe. Simply having a couple of students sit quietly and wait for separate instructions can work wonders. Taking a small group aside and asking them to make a choice can be very powerful. Adjusting seating arrangements or having a student sit next to a teacher can also have a significant impact. However, in some cases, administrators seemed to interpret the idea of "teaching the whole child" as a mandate to avoid imposing any consequences. I understand that stress was pervasive, and I was certainly feeling it, too. Our administrators likely had it even tougher. While this situation occurred at one school out of over fifty we visited, its effects were profound, impacting every student and staff member in that building.

Our administrators were navigating the same tumultuous changes, but they were the linchpin, the leaders. I've been a head coach before, and I know it's a challenging role. The administration was essentially our head coach during this period, and they must have been under immense stress. Considering the size of our school district, the impact of administrators varied. The effective ones were truly exceptional, bolstering their teachers, while the less effective ones left teachers feeling abandoned. My team and I witnessed these differences firsthand as we moved from school to school. You could almost sense it as you entered each building, right from the front office staff. Schools that had a well-structured approach in place were faring much better than those without it.

Throughout this period, I believed that our students would be okay. Whether during virtual learning, the hybrid model, or the return to in-person school, I thought they'd eventually adjust. I still hold onto that belief, thinking that this experience will ultimately shape them and make them stronger. However, I also came to realize that our students weren't okay. The seventeen months of disruptions had taken a significant toll on them, and they needed substantial support.

Our team continued running sixth-grade trips until November 19th, after which we switched back to fifth-grade trips. These had been shortened to one-day trips, running from December 7th until March 18th. On March 23rd, we transitioned back to sixth graders and finished out the year. Additionally, one of our team members fell ill in November and didn't return to our team. It wasn't until January that we got a long-term substitute. We were stretched to our limits, feeling the weight of stress and understaffing. It was challenging to remain composed and reflect on our experiences, let alone make substantial changes.

It took me months to fully comprehend what was happening, as I tend to be slow in grasping such matters. But eventually, I got there. I started addressing my class as a team, emphasizing that the better the team worked together, the more opportunities we'd all have. Students were either contributing to the team's success or hindering it. This concept helped eliminate almost all of my problems or made them significantly easier to manage. I could simply ask the student if their actions were benefiting the team, and it made a tremendous difference.

Part 2 - The Changes and Challenges Students Faced

Upon returning to school, our students had to wear masks, and let's face it, the masks weren't pleasant. They were uncomfortable, causing discomfort to everyone's ears, and they would often get dirty and emit unpleasant odors. It was far from enjoyable. Fortunately, we could take them off when we were outside. Masks had become a contentious topic, and our students had to navigate through the ongoing debate.

Some people even argued that masks "couldn't stop a fart, so how could they possibly stop a virus?" I understand that people had reservations about wearing masks, as I did too. However, I was willing to wear one to protect others. Many individuals were so frustrated that they were actively seeking reasons to stop wearing masks, and they weren't shy about expressing their opinions on social media and other platforms.

In hindsight, it's clear that this argument comparing smells and virus particles was flawed. The smell associated with a fart is caused by Hydrogen Sulfide, a molecule consisting of only three atoms bonded together. In contrast, the coronavirus is composed of roughly 200 million atoms bonded together. To put it in perspective, imagine your fart smell as three balloons tied together, the coronavirus as roughly 200 million balloons tied together, and your mask as the roof and walls protecting a large office building, with you being the building. Can three balloons make their way into your office building through the doors or windows? Possibly. Can roughly 200 million balloons tied together pass through those doors or windows? Absolutely not. But this was the logic that social media used to portray and rally anti-maskers. Frustrated adults looking for a way out made it even more challenging for our kids to process information.

To be fair to the anti-maskers, the information from the beginning was flawed. Some masks are way better than others. If the information about sunlight destroying the virus is accurate, you should never have to wear a mask outside. Our state leader was great, his rules made sense to me over

90% of the time. If the anti-maskers are right and I am wrong, the worst problem I caused was my ears hurt. If the pro-mask people are right and the anti-maskers are wrong, then we could be spreading the virus to at-risk people, making them really sick or worse. I was willing to take one for the team on this.

Not all parents wanted their kids wearing masks. So, they used thinner masks, made out of different materials. Bigger holes, worse filters. Now imagine being a student that was told they have to be careful. Maybe their mom is in a high-risk group, and they're told they need to wear their mask. They go to school and have to sit next to a kid whose parents hate masks and gave their kids a shirt sleeve to wear as a mask. Now the kids have to figure out who is right and how to live up to their parents' expectations. It is a horrible situation we put these kids in.

Our students also had to adapt to a new normal that included seating charts on buses, social distancing, contact tracing, self-reporting, vaccines, and copious amounts of hand sanitizer. They were once again required to remember the old rules while adjusting to the new ones.

It's important to remember that seventeen months ago my sixth graders were fourth graders who were just beginning to understand concepts of fairness, engage in cooperative play through small games, develop problem-solving skills, and learn about sportsmanship. They were also exploring their identities, enjoying body function humor, and working on expressing their emotions and anger. We effectively isolated them from their peers for over a year and expected all these social and emotional aspects of their development to somehow resolve themselves when we reopened schools.

On top of all these changes, the school had new expectations, and everyone was stressed. Many of us teachers overlooked the importance of reteaching expectations, routines, and appropriate behavior. We needed to embrace the role of kindergarten teachers to provide our students with the structure, expectations, and consequences they needed to navigate these changes. Regrettably, I didn't fully grasp this until a few trips into the school year, as I was just trying to survive and process everything that was changing. Many of our students were in the same boat.

Adding to the complexity were the vaccines. Adult vaccines were released on December 14th, 2020, and the unprecedented speed and new technology raised concerns for many, myself included. However, my wife and I got vaccinated as soon as we could. The vaccine became available to 12–15-year-olds on May 10th, 2021, but some people were resistant to the idea. We made the decision to vaccinate our oldest daughter as soon as possible. Then, on October 29th, the FDA approved the vaccine for 5–11-year-olds, and we vaccinated our youngest. It was a family decision made after thorough discussion and trust in medical experts.

However, misinformation and fake news began to dominate the narrative. Opinions were being presented as facts, and navigating the social media landscape was akin to traversing a treacherous swamp of information. Even as someone who had studied science for over three decades, I was shocked by the amount of misinformation out there. It was challenging for me to navigate between news and opinions. I was frustrated.

Our students had to process all of this too.

Returning to school also meant giving up the freedoms our students had become accustomed to while learning from home. They were bewildered by the need to ask for permission to use the bathroom, adhere to specific eating schedules, abstain from listening to music, and maintain a work schedule dictated by the bell. Coming back to school marked a significant cultural, social, and behavioral shift, and it was a lot to adjust to.

Part 3 - How My Family Reacted and Adapted

During this challenging period, I found myself stressed, exhausted, and struggling to take care of everyone. The physical toll of my stress was becoming evident as I gained weight and continued to experience hip pain. I became quick to lose my temper at home, and the laughter and smiles that used to fill our household became rare. I was wrestling with depression, and I knew that I needed to prioritize self-care, but finding the time and energy to do so was a daunting task.

I felt overwhelmed by worries about my job, my kids, my wife, and the frustration I harbored toward those who seemed to blame educators like me for all the changes in public schools. I was also disheartened by the perceived shortcomings of our leaders, and the weight of these concerns was mentally crushing me.

My wife was in a similar state of stress and exhaustion. Her work was taking a significant toll on her health, with migraines becoming a daily occurrence. The demands of her students seemed insurmountable; no matter how much she gave, people continued to ask for more.

Eventually, we made the difficult decision for her to step away from teaching. It was a challenging choice, but ultimately, it was the right one for our family's well-being. We knew we had to adapt our lifestyle, even though it meant a significant reduction in our income. However, the decision proved immensely beneficial for our family.

Our daughters were also struggling during this time, and they needed attention, guidance, and support. It was difficult to discern their pain when they remained quiet. My wife worked closely with both girls and, to our surprise, discovered just how deeply they had been affected. I recall many tearful moments from all of us during this period. Hugs and expressions of love became essential as we focused on nurturing our most important community: our family.

Navigating this process was incredibly challenging. We had to learn to slow down and express our feelings, foster independence, discover our identities, communicate our anger and frustration, and manage the ongoing stress. I vividly remember my wife's last day of work. While we were both excited about this new chapter, I took a moment to tell her, "You know, it's okay if you wake up tomorrow and you don't feel great." She was taken aback and asked, "What do you mean?" My intention was to let her know that it takes time to process and heal from stress. I emphasized that it might take months or even years. I just wanted to help her manage her expectations, and I'm grateful that I did.

My oldest daughter faced challenges adjusting to the classroom environment. Her two best friends had left the school, leaving her struggling to find a new friend group. Lunchtime became a significant source of stress for her as she grappled with the decision of where to sit. The situation worsened when the school began having lunch outside, where most of her friends were more interested in playing football. Once again, she found herself without a solid friend group.

Additionally, the school implemented a requirement for teachers to use one digital platform for posting assignments. Unfortunately, not all teachers were proficient in using the platform or organizing it effectively. This inconsistency in digital classroom organization became a frustrating aspect of her school experience.

My oldest daughter tends to work slowly on assignments, especially when there are distractions. Online, she was able to complete her work and achieve excellent scores. However, there was an expectation for her to excel academically as the teacher's daughter. She was sacrificing her recess to complete assignments, and both her teachers and peers made subtle comments about her work habits. These small wounds still sting today.

She began feeling like a disappointment, and each comment felt like a mosquito bite. When she finally opened up about her struggles, it was clear that she was emotionally overwhelmed. My once amazing, smart, silly, and wonderful daughter had suffered a significant blow to her mental well-being. Her self-image had been shaken, and she struggled to recognize all the remarkable qualities she possessed. Her confidence and self-esteem had taken a hit, and I still harbor some frustration toward a few of her peers and teachers who contributed to her distress.

My youngest daughter was grappling with different anxieties. She was entering sixth grade at her school, where fourth, fifth, and sixth graders shared the same classroom, and sixth graders were expected to take on leadership roles. She had only spent seven months in the classroom, took a seventeen-month hiatus, and was now required to step into a leadership position. She didn't remember everything, and she was afraid of making mistakes.

Just before the school year began, she changed her hairstyle, which was another adjustment for her. She also had to cope with losing friends and making new ones. Being around real people felt strange to her after the extended period of remote learning. She found the fourth graders to be quite immature, with lots of conflicts and tears. Hearing her classmates not showing interest in reading was surprising and disappointing to her. Her class held weekly community meetings, but she described them as chaotic, often taking much longer than necessary, with her classmates struggling to manage the process.

Despite these challenges, her horseback riding was going well, and she had opportunities to hang out with friends. As the school year progressed, she began enjoying being back in the school environment.

Then another blow struck when my wife's dad fell ill. We traveled to Florida to visit and spend quality time with his family. After recently losing my mom, I was determined to ensure my wife enjoyed every precious moment she could with her dad. When we arrived, we noticed that one of his legs was swollen, but he was still trying to maintain his usual activities. Despite the underlying concern, we had a wonderful trip filled with cherished memories. We traveled to the beach to watch the sunset. We spent time with family. We played games and enjoyed being with each other.

One unforgettable moment was when all the girls and my wife's dad sang karaoke together in the living room. The disco ball was on, the lights were low, and they were all dancing and singing, "Oh What a Night!"

We only grasped the gravity of the situation upon our return. His test results came back positive for cancer, and tragically, he passed away just three weeks later.

Losing my wife's dad was sudden and deeply painful. Coping with such a loss was incredibly challenging, and each of us seemed to process it in our own unique way. We returned to Florida for the funeral to find closure and support.

As the school year came to an end, I felt utterly drained. I couldn't relax, and the stress seemed to cling to me. Despite positive developments, such as hiring a new staff member, having a full team again, good health all around, and the pandemic being behind us, I couldn't let go of the stress.

We have hit a point in our lives as teachers were we don't have to work over the summer unless we choose it. I like to do workshops, but I was done. We are lucky enough to have my wife's mom rent a home on the Outer Banks for the whole family. We get to take a week off and just enjoy being present. Her mom does most of the meal planning and cooking. Our kids get up early to hang out with Grandma and Grandpa. I have to make a meal and help with little things, but it is a true vacation. I am not making any big decisions.

About halfway through the week, on Thursday July 7th, as I sat on the beach, I experienced a true moment of peace. I love the ocean. I love the waves, the smell, the sounds, the birds, I love it all. Sitting in my chair, watching the waves build and crash, I let go. Like releasing a deep breath, I settled into the present. I let some of the past go enough to enjoy the moment. Watching the waves move in and out I finally relaxed. I didn't know how tense I was until I let go. Like working out and holding your breath, you don't realize it until you cannot breathe. That first breath is a reminder. It grounds you. I finally felt that release. It was as if a wave of calm swept over my body, allowing me to take a deep breath and find some peace.

Chapter 6
No Masks, No Pandemic, What Could Go Wrong?

As the summer drew to a close, I felt better. We had a trip with our friends to Yellowstone and Glacier National Park. We were able to see bears, moose and mountain goats. But my fuse was short, I was still stressed, I was still dealing with the chaos of the pandemic. We got a new team member and I was excited to work with him.

The process of bringing a fresh face on board was filled with excitement, as new people inject a vibrant energy into the mix. With a school district boasting numerous exceptional teachers, I had no doubt that our latest addition would strengthen our team. Moreover, this new member's arrival meant I was no longer the newcomer, which was a cool novelty.

Returning to work was something I looked forward to, despite the fact that I was still grappling with stress and lingering frustration, clinging to old grievances. My patience for thoughtless actions and complaints had worn thin, and I sensed I had reached my limit. During such moments, I found solace in the pages of one of my favorite books, *Faith of the Fallen* by Terry Goodkind.

In this book, the main character, Richard, finds himself in dire circumstances, having lost everything. However, as the story unfolds, he resolves to make the most of every second. He builds communities and forms friendships, confounding his captor, who expected him to give up.

One of the most remarkable chapters involves a confrontation with a young thug. Instead of cowering, Richard stands up to him and even feels compassion for this young man.

This thug, blinded by his perceived power, is unable to comprehend Richard's perspective. Richard implores this young man to embrace life, stressing that he only has one life, and he should live it to the fullest. He encourages the young man to take pride in himself and his surroundings and teaches him to improve their apartment complex. Soon everyone in the building joins in to clean and make repairs (Goodkind, 520-525).

The entire book is marked by such inspiring moments until one day when the main character hits rock bottom. He goes to bed despondent, ready to give up, but he wakes up the next morning with renewed purpose and determination.

Every time I read this, I want to be like him. I want to have the vision to see the good and the determination to make it happen.

Though I still felt broken after the summer, I was slightly better than I had been at the end of the school year. Training a new teacher held an exciting promise, offering something to look forward to. A pep talk with my favorite book strengthened my resolve, and I was determined to make the most of the upcoming school year.

My patience was gone, but simultaneously, I felt a sense of excitement as things were heading in the right direction. My wife was actively seeking a new job. Meanwhile, my eldest child was gearing up for high school and, having just completed her hockey camp, was eagerly anticipating the new academic year. My youngest, about to enter seventh grade, had wrapped up her horseback riding camp and was looking forward to school and reconnecting with friends.

Part 1 - Me and My Job

I wasn't exactly recharged, but I was eagerly anticipating the start of the new school year. Our team was going to consist of four teachers once again, and we were gearing up to organize full trips for both sixth and fifth graders. The prospect of working with students in normal conditions was promising, but as it turned out, things weren't going to be as smooth as we'd hoped.

School commenced on August 17th, 2022, and our first field trip was scheduled for August 24th. While the students were showing improvement, many of them were still broken. Fortunately, a good number of them remembered us, and the teacher we collaborated with initially was nothing short of amazing. Her meticulous organization ensured that students understood her expectations, and the cafeteria experience was remarkably smooth. The first few trips were relatively small, allowing us to acclimate our new teacher to the routine, which turned out to be quite enjoyable.

The bus, however, presented a new environment for many of these students, and we continued to encounter issues with some of them seeking attention and causing disruptions. Most could not put down windows, they would interrupt directions, and they would ask ridiculous questions. "What happens if we die? What happens if we get eaten by a bear? What happens if an eagle flies in the window?" I started calling it the "what if" game.

After a year of grappling with these challenging students, I decided to change my approach. I began emphasizing the importance of time management, highlighting how every distraction not only disrupted our team but also affected our entire community.

When a student attempted to grab everyone's attention inappropriately, I would calmly remind them that their actions were undermining our sense of community and ask if that was their intention. This approach, though it required occasional reinforcement, proved to be quite effective. On the flip side, the students were eager to engage with me, sharing their interests and stories. They excelled in one-on-one interactions and small groups, but large gatherings, such as bus rides and lunchtime, often started as a hot mess.

During lunch breaks, our students would clamor for food, eat for a mere two minutes, and then spend the next fifteen minutes running around. It was both baffling and surprising. In the pre-pandemic era, students used to sit and eat lunch. Last year, they were still adapting to wearing masks most of the time, and social distancing was the norm. They didn't appear as frenzied during lunch back then. However, this year, they seemed determined to make up for the past two years of isolation in a single lunch period. It was reminiscent of the chaos that unfolds when new dogs are introduced to a dog park—they go wild for about fifteen to twenty minutes before settling down. Lunchtime mirrored this pattern precisely. Every time a new student joined a group, the social dynamics had to be reestablished, with attention serving as the coveted currency. The result was escalating screams and competing for attention.

Something as simple as managing noise levels, which used to be effortless pre-pandemic, became a source of potential chaos during the 2022-2023 school year. I wanted my students to enjoy themselves, become attuned to their environment, and even experience the thrill of an echoing voice, but they did know when it was appropriate to scream. They screamed constantly.

When I approached the students to address this behavior, they were genuinely shocked. They couldn't comprehend why screaming at the top of their lungs was problematic, or why they couldn't cling to their friends. Most students were receptive and tried to follow the rules once they understood the reasoning behind them. This necessitated incorporating these rules into my guidelines. I posed the question: "If there's an emergency, and I need to relay important information to you, can I do that effectively if you're all screaming?" The answer was a resounding "No." Thus, we agreed to save our vocal enthusiasm for appropriate times, seeking opportunities to let them release their energy constructively.

While some groups responded to our reteaching beautifully, others struggled, and I had the challenging task of building a two-day learning community with over 82 different student groups, consistently dealing with the issues of screaming and excessive physical contact. They had no physical boundaries, they wanted to sit on each other's laps, hang on to each other and pet each other.

Candy during lunchtime presented another major challenge. I recall one incident at a particular school where students brought backpacks filled with candy. They would hold up a snack and shout, "Who wants Starbursts?" The result? A chaotic rush of students toward the student with the candy. Instead of allowing the student to distribute the sweets, they grabbed it out of the student's hands. As a result, we had to confiscate all the candy and return it to the original owners at the end of the day. In my 12 years of teaching outdoor school, this was a first.

Typically, students would ask if they could share, and we would politely decline. However, this particular student's attempt to grab attention through food backfired, leaving this student shocked that their classmates would resort to such behavior as attacking and stealing their food. The student was shocked; we were shocked.

This is Playground Etiquette 101. We've all witnessed a child having to share his entire pack of gum because they brought it out in front of a group, or, worse yet, we've been that child ourselves. It's a lesson that typically only needs to be learned once. However, in this case, the student seemed utterly clueless. He had no inkling of what was about to transpire, and honestly, neither did we. Managing 60-100 rambunctious kids and restoring order after a miniature food riot is no small feat. Regrettably, we lost half of our afternoon activities due to the time it took to address this one incident.

We had to revise our message once more. We asked them, "Do you want an extended lunch?" If the answer was yes, we encouraged them to finish eating and then sit quietly while engaging in conversation with their friends. We explained that if they remained quiet, it would appear to my boss that they were still eating, resulting in a longer lunch break. Sometimes it worked, but there were occasions when it didn't.

Another challenge was students forgetting how to clean up after themselves. Very few groups managed to clean up on their first attempt. Even though we were teaching them about the environment, biodiversity, and resources, many students didn't grasp why disposing of their trash was so important. Despite explaining the connections, a significant portion of them remained reluctant to clean up after themselves.

This is a basic expectation taught at home and in every grade at school – clean up and put things away. For some students, it proved to be too demanding. We had to make groups stay seated until they were dismissed to ensure accountability. Before the pandemic, students typically knew what was expected and would clean up when asked, but during this school year, it felt like pulling teeth for a larger percentage of them. For some groups, it looked like they dumped their whole lunch box on the ground and just walked away. No one cared. My team and the parents were shocked, and we had to wrap our minds around this. Yes, we all have to clean up our mess!

The issue of excessive screaming on the bus persisted throughout the year. I found myself constantly reminding students that it was inappropriate to scream at every bump the bus went over, emphasizing that such behavior disrupted the sense of community we were trying to foster. This became a mentally exhausting routine, occurring on every trip, at several bumps in the road, and at each significant railroad crossing.

On the positive side, I was forging connections with our students through storytelling, and they were opening up to share their hopes and dreams. We had the opportunity to discover salamanders, frogs, insects, crayfish, and, with one group, we even spotted a bear. For most students, these experiences were highly enjoyable and needed. Many had developed a fear of the outdoors, the unknown, and nature itself.

Part 2 - The Changes and Challenges Students Faced

Returning to school in 2022 brought significant changes, marking the first normal start since 2019 and the first uninterrupted school year in three years. However, "normal" was a relative term, as our school district grappled with severe staffing shortages. We had unfilled bus routes and a shortage of support staff, and this translated into emergency teachers, larger class sizes, and a revolving door of educators. The overall situation was chaotic, exacerbated by the mounting stress levels, causing some educators to leave the profession mid-year.

Maintaining structure is a challenge when a new teacher arrives each month; trust is difficult to establish amidst constant change and settling into a routine seemed elusive when the core pieces remained in flux. Yet our students had to adapt to these circumstances, and regrettably, many of them, including my oldest daughter, were affected.

Students also had to contend with stricter rules, as the administration system-wide began to hold them more accountable for their actions. This was particularly jarring for a small percentage of students who had been accustomed to doing as they pleased. Additionally, teaching became more focused on meeting educational standards, which came as a surprise to me because I was under the assumption that it had always been that way. Efforts were made to ensure that teachers were aligning their instruction with these standards.

Furthermore, students had the added pressure of receiving their standardized test results for the 2020-2021 school year, the 2021-2022 school year, and the 2022-2023 school year. The state held them accountable for these results. These were among the most challenging years of teaching, given the pandemic-related disruptions, and yet, our state expected students to perform according to these standards.

My county made a commendable collective effort, but I had reservations about holding students accountable for standardized tests during the midst and aftermath of a pandemic. This was a decision mandated at the state and federal levels, tied to funding. I wished that the resources expended on these tests could have been directed toward more meaningful support. These tests cost millions of dollars to buy and administer. Imagine if we used that money to hire more teachers, counselors, and support staff. For every million we spend on testing, we could hire 20 more teachers.

In my estimation, approximately 10% of students consistently excel, often due to strong parental support and financial resources, while another 10% constantly struggle or may choose to fail. The remaining 80% fluctuates based on a multitude of factors, relying on numerous nudges and interventions when needed. Success also hinges on their willingness to accept help when it's offered. I personally identify with being part of this 80%, as I don't always accept help, but I do often enough to achieve success.

This is just my observation over the years. I know the top students will almost always be successful. I know the bottom needs to hit the bottom to change. They can, and some do, but most are still trying to find the bottom. That means teachers should focus on the 80% they can impact. These are the students that need the praise, or push, or encouragement. I teach everyone that steps into my classroom, but that middle 80% is the group I feel like I have the greatest impact on. The right word at the right time can elevate and inspire students, the wrong word or feedback can crush them, and we decided to hold them accountable to standardized tests taken during the pandemic. Ouch!

Amidst these challenges, students were still navigating the complexities of social rules, forging their sense of identity, establishing peer groups, and developing their moral compass. They found themselves making mistakes typically associated with early elementary school, yet they were now in middle or high school. High school students were grappling with the social intricacies of both middle school and high school simultaneously, while middle school students were adapting to elementary school etiquette within a middle school setting. Elementary school students, on the other hand, were grappling with missing out on kindergarten and first-grade experiences. The social and developmental gaps were significant.

These social stresses coincided with the increased academic expectations, and in hindsight, it was a substantial burden for them to bear.

In the 2022-2023 school year, students from urban and rural areas displayed strikingly similar behaviors. Large groups posed a challenge, with any attention holding immense importance. It often seemed like a massive game of who is going to lose it, with students screaming, taunting and hanging on to each other until someone had enough and lost their cool.

In contrast, my personal observations of suburban students suggested they were better adjusted. One possible explanation is that they experienced fewer losses during the pandemic. They belonged to various clubs, had numerous hobbies, and had friends nearby. Their parents engaged with neighbors in social settings, making peer gatherings more accessible. They only missed out on their communities for a brief period, whereas city and country students faced prolonged isolation. They lost their playground, but they got it back the quickest.

Although both urban and rural students eventually resumed their sports and clubs, the initial delay took a toll. Many urban students relied heavily on school groups and clubs, similarly to rural students who had limited options due to their small population density and remote locations, making it difficult to see their friends.

Perhaps it was a sense of hopelessness that led to these behaviors. Both groups had experienced high-profile news stories filled with violence that negatively impacted them. Understanding their shared struggles is the first step towards addressing this issue. While it may take years to unravel the root causes, having a starting point allows us to work together towards a more positive future. This is where we currently stand, and this is where we aim to be — let's embark on this journey together.

Part 3 - How My Family Reacted and Adapted

I decided to have a heart-to-heart conversation with my daughters about the past three years, turning it into an interview of sorts where I asked questions and took notes. It turned out to be a deeply rewarding experience, offering insights and moments of sadness. I highly recommend it. Much like me, they struggled to recall all the details at first, but as we conversed, memories began to resurface. We found ourselves hopping around our timeline, attempting to piece together events in the correct order. The exercise proved valuable as we discovered that we viewed similar things as being positive and faced some of the same challenges.

Both of my daughters felt that the 2022-2023 school year was "normal." My younger daughter started 7th grade, her first year of middle school, at a charter school, sharing a classroom with 8th graders. She was initially quite apprehensive. Despite her love for most of the group work they were doing, she underwent several shifts in friend groups. She was taken aback by the unkindness displayed by her friends toward each other, particularly one friend who was consistently mean. While she was aware of her friend's meanness, she was shocked by how people reacted when subjected to it. Her friends would isolate this student and exclude her; she was being shunned by the group. They turned on her and treated her badly because she was treating people badly. This made no sense to my daughter, but it is the application of the "Golden Rule." She is being mean to us so, she must want us to be mean to her.

She had other friends she genuinely liked, and she tried to bring them all together, but this often resulted in the group targeting the socially weakest member. My youngest daughter was deeply disturbed by how they treated each other, and she spoke about three significant changes within her friend group. Three times the group shuffled members.

My younger daughter is remarkably independent and strong-willed. She adores books and can easily entertain herself. We would check on her, and she'd assure us that everything was fine—until it wasn't. By February, visible signs of stress began to manifest, and her smile disappeared. We could tell that she didn't want to burden us with her worries. Even activities she used to enjoy, like horseback riding, had lost their appeal. The entire family felt the strain. I recall entering her room one day, giving her an encouraging pep talk, and holding her while she cried. It was a heart-wrenching moment.

The pep talk seemed to offer some relief, but the following weeks remained stressful, possibly coinciding with the second significant change in her friend group. However, her third set of friends appeared to be the best fit. They shared books, collaborated on class projects, and even worked together on a classroom economy project. She began to bounce back, and the classroom economy funded a school dance, which she and her classmates planned. It turned out to be the highlight of her school year.

I was initially a little frustrated by the inconvenience of having to purchase a dress and organize transportation to the dance, but we went through with it. Another parent graciously hosted the girls at her home to get ready, and it was a fantastic experience. Such a simple idea had a profound impact. My youngest daughter was overjoyed. We all gathered at the school for photos, and the atmosphere was electric. Witnessing your child's excitement is profoundly moving. Everyone was dressed up and thrilled about the dance. We captured photos of everyone singing and dancing throughout the night. It was a truly wonderful way to conclude the school year.

Meanwhile, my oldest daughter was embarking on high school, a source of immense stress as she was essentially starting over. Her transition from a small charter school to a public high school was a notable change. In her former school, everyone knew each other, but in her new environment, she knew only a few students. She had to navigate her way through this unfamiliar territory. During the initial week, she found herself without anyone to sit with during lunch. As parents, we reached out to connect her with potential lunch buddies, and fortunately, this effort paid off, and she began making new friends.

With the return of sports, my oldest expressed a desire to attend the first home football game. We attended the game as a family, allowing her to spend time with friends. Her friend was part of the JV football team. They hung out in the student section of the stadium, and we were seated with other families in the stands. At the time, her team was winning.

Then a fight suddenly broke out in the stands. I was seated about 30 yards away from where the altercation began. Drawing from my experience of working at high school events over the years, I recognized that such incidents, while regrettable, occasionally occurred. This particular fight involved two young girls, and it turned out to be quite violent, as girl fights often tend to be.

In my experience, when a crowd forms, it's typically the first sign that something undesirable is happening. Students gather, which attracts teachers and administrators, and the situation is usually diffused swiftly. However, in this case, that wasn't the outcome. The fight commenced, and onlookers watched for about 10-20 seconds before a parent from the stands intervened and broke it up. One of the girls involved was taken to the administrators while teachers and game staff arrived on the scene. Strangely, instead of dispersing, the crowd's energy escalated, with increased screaming and shouting. Police lights appeared, and then the entire crowd scattered. Consequently, the football game was halted, and the stadium was evacuated.

In the midst of all this chaos, I had the added responsibility of locating my oldest daughter. My predominant emotion was anger rather than fear, as I was essentially watching a pot boil. I had seen it before and had certain expectations about it. I was particularly displeased by the panic that the students caused. It only took one student and a follower to disrupt the entire game. One student screamed something stupid, and their friend panicked. Then everyone nearby panicked. Panic is contagious.

This pattern was distressingly familiar to me, as it mirrored what was happening on my bus every day. Whether it was a bump in the road, a bee flying in through a window, or a loud noise caused by a water bottle hitting the floor, the immediate response of a large group of students was to panic and scream at the top of their lungs.

Many parents, myself included, were understandably upset about the events at the football game. I did not blame the staff; I recognized that the middle school students attending the game were responsible for the chaos. Fortunately, the school implemented a solution for the next home game by requiring every student under sixteen to be accompanied by an adult. This simple, effective measure demonstrated the power of parental supervision.

As my oldest daughter continued to navigate high school, she maintained good grades despite experiencing staffing issues. Her math teacher had to leave due to a family emergency, and unfortunately, the school struggled to find a replacement. Another teacher with a full schedule temporarily took over the class, and this arrangement lasted for about a month before she received a new teacher. It was certainly not an ideal situation.

When basketball season rolled around, my oldest daughter had formed a solid friend group, and they attended nearly all the home basketball games, which was a positive development. The team's performance was great, and things were generally looking up, with one notable exception – her science class. I had allowed her to choose her class, a decision I regret deeply.

When picking classes and preparing to start the school year, she was adamant about not wanting to hear any advice from her parents, believing she could figure it all out on her own. This proved to be a challenge for me, given my 15 years of teaching high school and my previous role as the science department chair. I possessed a wealth of knowledge to guide her in choosing classes and preparing for her future, yet all she would say was that my advice didn't apply to her.

I know that some students need to do things their way first, and my oldest daughter is certainly one of those students. I allowed her that independence, even though I wish I hadn't. She picked her classes and resisted the leveling process. If I had known that she was carrying the mental baggage of her friends and classmates and feeling like a disappointment, I could have offered better guidance. I didn't realize the extent of the hurtful comments she was internalizing; I merely assumed she was being stubborn.

This was undoubtedly a significant lapse on my part. Rather than making a genuine effort to understand the situation, I found myself reacting solely to the surface information, which often led to anger. Subsequently, I adopted a "fine, do it your way" approach, which in hindsight, wasn't the most helpful response.

Withholding advice on all aspects of high school was difficult for me, but seeing how this lack of guidance affected the quality of her science class was particularly heart-wrenching; I have a deep passion for the subject and believe it to be incredibly enriching. Unfortunately, her experience in this class did not align with my expectations. While I'm no longer in a classroom every day, I know that teaching can be a challenging task. Nonetheless, it seemed to me that her class was falling far short of providing her with an enriching science education.

My oldest also encountered some challenges with homework, but she eventually found her way, with my wife and I providing support. Mostly my wife. I had to shift my perspective and understand that she needed guidance rather than quick fixes. Once I grasped this concept, helping her became a smoother and more productive process for both of us.

At the beginning of the school year, my wife took on the role of a full-time mom, which was a wonderful arrangement for our family. She could manage our children's activities, stay on top of schoolwork, and offer tremendous support to our daughters. She also began the search for a new job that would be the right fit, although finding such a job proved to be a challenging endeavor and took several months. Finally, around mid-December, she secured a job creating online lessons, a role that truly suited her.

Her ability to break down and explain complex topics is a superpower, and her departure from classroom teaching was a significant loss for our school system. However, she found great value in writing online lessons, and by December, she began to feel better. It had been nearly a year since she had stopped working for the school district, and she was now able to observe the positive impact this decision had on our family.

Consider this: a whole year had passed since my wife stopped teaching. She could now look at each of us and see the effects of the pandemic. Every day she was inquiring about our well-being, acting as our lifeguard. Her love for us was so profound that she acknowledged the challenges we were facing and expressed a strong desire to help us overcome them. She had essentially been one year ahead of the rest of us in recognizing the extent of our struggles. While working part-time, she devoted significant effort to bringing our family back together.

During all this, I was falling apart physically. At the end of the 2021 school year, I experienced a locked-up hip flexor, causing intense pain on my left side and limiting my ability to stand for more than 5-10 minutes at a time. In January 2022, I began physical therapy, but progress was slow, partly due to my failure to consistently perform the recommended at-home exercises. By July 2022, I had started working out at home and was beginning to feel better, until I injured my ribs in November, leading me to discontinue my workouts.

This injury felt like the last straw for me. I was under immense stress at work, my physical and mental well-being were deteriorating, and my oldest daughter was in the midst of a rebellion, searching for her identity. Amid it all, a heated argument erupted between my wife and me over my oldest daughter's homecoming dress, resulting in hurtful words being exchanged that pushed me to my breaking point. I needed to escape, so I got into my car and began driving with no plan or destination, simply in search of some space to process everything.

As I drove north, I called my dad, who has always been there for me through thick and thin. He's been a great source of support throughout my life, and he was wonderful during that phone call. He listened attentively as I explained my feelings, and though he didn't have all the answers I needed, he tried to suggest places where I might find them. After our conversation, I began to think about my wife and daughters and what I wanted our future to look like. I realized I needed to return home.

That night, I broke down. I recognized that I don't have all the answers, nor am I a superhero. I'm just trying my best to navigate an incredibly challenging situation. I love my family dearly and it's frustrating that something as trivial as a red dress pushed me over the edge. I'm deeply ashamed that I left the house that night, and I deeply regret my impulsive decision to drive away. At that moment, I felt like a speck of cosmic dust adrift in the vastness of space, scorching hot on one side and frozen on the other.

I adore my oldest daughter. I cherish her smile, her songs, her wit, her artistic talents, and watching her play ice hockey. I want nothing but the best for her. However, I don't approve of roughly 25% of her wardrobe choices. It's challenging to convey how risky I believe her behavior to be. In an ideal world, individuals should have the freedom to dress however they please, but our world is far from perfect, and every choice carries risks. The way we dress sends a message, and we all know the saying, "dress for success."

People judge us based on our attire and appearance, and my daughter is not exempt from this scrutiny. At 15, she looks like she's in her mid-twenties, often turning heads in public. I worry that she's just one catcall away from a mental and emotional breaking point. Negative attention, driven by short-term desire and lust, is not the same as positive attention based on respect and getting to know someone.

I don't want either of my daughters to become victims. I am not saying that she is asking to become a victim. I am saying she doesn't understand how much attention she is attracting. The more people that notice you, the more likely it is that you will attract the attention of a dangerous person. I realize she could attract the attention of a dangerous person while she is dressed head to toe in winter clothes. I realize that dangerous people might not be attracted to clothes at all, maybe it is hair, or facial expressions, or just being in the wrong place at the wrong time. I fight this battle in my mind and sometimes I lose. My mind thinks I can protect her if I say something, but I am learning; I am trying to respect my daughter's choices and protect her from all the bad people I picture in my head.

I love my daughter, and I want her to be able to express herself and dress how she feels comfortable. I also want to protect my baby. I don't know how to navigate this. I am still trying. I know that I am not comfortable with what she wears some days. She is not always comfortable with what I wear either. I only want to protect her, as most parents do.

She has experienced mental abuse from friends and teachers, with lingering backhanded insults about her work habits. Imagine these insults directed at her body and clothing choices. We know how destructive such comments can be, and it's important to consider an article on usafacts.org, published on March 15th, 2023, which reveals that mental health among high school teens is deteriorating, with one of the highest rates of persistent depression and hopelessness according to a CDC report. As a parent of two teenagers, this is nothing short of terrifying. The thought of her being bullied, or worse, scares me so much it can sometimes feel debilitating.

A single thoughtless comment can haunt us for a lifetime, and I carry several such comments with me. I simply don't want my daughter to experience this kind of pain. I believe that wearing similar but slightly different clothes could help mitigate these risks, but I must express this concern very carefully. In the past, I didn't consider my tone, and now my family views me as the bad guy for voicing my concerns. It's maddening to be met with a lack of understanding when I'm only trying to protect my daughter. I'm filled with anger, concern, and fear, but my family refuses to listen because of the emotions I bring to the conversation. I hope more than anything, that as my daughter grows and finds friends, she starts to prioritize genuine positive attention. I hope she finds a balance of dressing to feel confident and dressing to feel beautiful that is closer to my own ideas of what those things should look like. I hope that my quest to guide her and steer her in the right direction is positive. I don't know anything; I just love her like only a parent can.

My wife and I eventually had a productive conversation about the situation. It took some time for both of us to calm down. I reduced how frequently I expressed my concerns about our daughter's clothing choices, and when I did bring it up, I made an effort to change my tone. More often than not, my daughter listened and responded positively.

In January, I contracted COVID-19, which meant that three out of four family members had been infected. Surprisingly, my youngest never tested positive for the virus. I was bedridden for a week and faced another challenge about a month later when I experienced severe vertigo, which made me fear for my life. I got up in the middle of the night and almost fell when I tried to walk to the bathroom. It was so bad I wanted to puke.

About a month after that, I had another bout of vertigo. Dealing with vertigo was incredibly challenging. You have crystals in your semicircular canals in your ear; every now and then they move, and you have to put them back by doing the Epley maneuver. I considered it the final straw and realized that I needed to prioritize my health and well-being. I required more than just temporary solutions; I needed long-term routines to get better and regain my health.

I managed to make it to the end of the school year, but it was a struggle. I had difficulty making even simple decisions, and this problem persists to some extent. Tasks like planning dinner or a family vacation seemed overwhelming. I needed a break, a reset button, and a chance to recharge during the summer. For a long time, I was reluctant to admit this, but the three years of the pandemic had taken a severe toll on me mentally and physically.

Summer break felt like a breath of fresh air. I had the freedom to do whatever I wanted. The first week was fantastic. I borrowed a kayak from a friend and spent time on the river. I enjoyed leisurely walks with my dog and reconnected with my hobbies, including organizing my collection of rocks. I was truly embracing life until I threw out my back, which sent me back to physical therapy. However, this time around, I managed to make time for the home workouts. Finally, I had the opportunity to slow down, take a deep breath, and process the events of the past three years.

I had several conversations with others about our students, and people were genuinely interested in the changes I had observed. They began to relate these experiences to their own children, and the discussions became exciting and engaging. This enthusiasm was contagious, and it inspired me to sit down and start writing. I thought that perhaps everyone was ready to take a deep breath, reflect on the past three years, and work together towards healing and recovery.

Chapter 7
You Are Not Alone

The lead-up to the summer of 2023 felt more like a sluggish crawl than a race. By March, I was utterly drained. Everything seemed insurmountable. Dinner? Nope, couldn't handle that. Laundry? Not a chance. Having fun? Sorry, but that was out of the question. Cleaning? Forget it. Planning a vacation? No way. Working out? Absolutely not. Hanging out with friends? Well, I'd do it, but I couldn't promise I'd be thrilled about it. Even waking up was a struggle – okay, fine, but only after hitting snooze a few times. I was truly at my breaking point. Decision fatigue had me in its suffocating grip.

Money was a constant source of stress. With my wife no longer working, we lost nearly half of our income, yet our expensive hobbies persisted. We were trying to save, but our efforts couldn't keep pace with the rising inflation. Spring break was on the horizon, but I wasn't convinced that going somewhere was a wise choice. Our usual destination was a trip south to visit my wife's late father. His passing still weighed heavily on her heart. While she had siblings and a stepmother down there, it just wasn't the same as having a dad. The thought of coming up with a new vacation idea felt overwhelming.

Finally, my wife and I made a decision – a family hiking trip. We discovered an affordable cabin near three popular hikes along the Appalachian Trail in Virginia, collectively known as "The Triple Crown." It sounded like an exciting adventure. Over three days, we conquered all three hikes. We walked a little over 25 miles, dining out in the evenings and enjoying a complete break from the outside world. Our phone signal was sporadic at best, and it was wonderful.

The woods had a profound impact on us. Being together in that environment was incredibly powerful, strengthening our bond as a family. We depended on one another for support, discovered new things together, and pushed our limits. It was a fantastic team-building experience with the people we trusted most – our family. Despite the initial intimidation of being in a new and daunting place, we had our emotional safety net. Our family was together. If you're a hiking enthusiast, I highly recommend looking up "The Triple Crown, Roanoke Virginia" – it won't disappoint.

Unfortunately, the break from work was too short-lived, and the stress immediately resurfaced when work resumed. The students hadn't magically transformed over spring break. Behavioral issues remained unresolved. The "Golden Rule" still eluded them, and they struggled to differentiate between real-life communities and their social media substitute. Their anxiety hadn't vanished, and they hadn't suddenly developed the ability to "read the room." They were still struggling.

While being isolated with my family had its challenges, it was also peaceful. Hiking was peaceful, as was having lunch atop a ridgeline, and even dinner conversations were filled with a different kind of quiet. A week of tranquility was shattered upon my return to work. All the stress I was able to forget about over the break came rushing back.

The final month of school felt similar to my experience in the last marathon I ran. I had trained diligently, completing all my runs and adequately preparing for the race. For the first 23 miles, my pace remained consistent, and I felt in control of the race, brimming with confidence. However, at mile 24, I suddenly cramped up, and the helplessness of having my body fail me was overwhelming. You never expect to push your body until it shuts down; we all believe our bodies will never fail us. But when they do, it feels like the ultimate betrayal.

My legs cramped up just as I caught sight of the Pentagon, and a mixture of anger, frustration, and sadness overwhelmed me. I could see the finish line, but I couldn't walk due to the muscle cramps. Each step was tentative, with potentially disastrous consequences. I attempted to stop, stretch, and try again, a cycle of walking, cramping, stretching, and repeating. To achieve my goal of finishing in under four hours, I needed to cover 2.2 miles in under 30 minutes. It took me over an hour to do so.

The final hundred feet of the race involved a hill lined with cheering Marines. Despite my severe leg cramps, their positive encouragement spurred me on to peg-leg run the last stretch, reminiscent of Forrest Gump in leg braces, except I had no braces, just agonizing leg cramps.

The last month of the school year felt like this; it seemed interminable, and I felt mentally exhausted. Reaching the last day was only possible because of the promise of summer break – the freedom from making decisions, redirecting students, enduring screams at every bump, and handling students who had seemingly forgotten how to work in groups.

My school district's early start in August allowed us to finish in early June, and I couldn't have been more excited. The last day of school felt like Christmas morning, the first bicycle ride without training wheels, or that first solo drive. The excitement and freedom were exhilarating. I focused on myself, allowing my daughters to do their own thing while my wife worked and supported us mentally and emotionally.

At the start of summer break, I admittedly indulged in selfishness. I spent most of my time exploring the river, which had been calling my name for months. I'd take the dog for walks and my daughters for swims along the river, but it wasn't enough. So, I began kayaking the river, which turned out to be a jackpot. Being alone on the water was exactly what I needed. During this time, I had the opportunity to reflect on the past three years, especially the challenges brought about by the pandemic. I thought about how I could help myself, my family, and my students. As the weeks passed, I had numerous conversations about my work, and I realized that others shared similar experiences. They relaxed when we discovered common ground, often remarking, "I thought it was just me." So, in case it hasn't fully sunk in yet, let's say it loud and clear: It's not just you; we're all in the same boat.

Part 1 - You Are Not Alone

One of the most common questions I receive from fellow teachers during our trips is, "How do my students compare? Is it like this everywhere?" The concise response is, "Yes, it's like this everywhere. Our students are broken." This understanding is crucial, and I want to emphasize: You are not alone. It's not just you, it is not just your students, it is not just your child. While some children are more affected than others, it's important to recognize that the scars run deep for everyone.

On the surface, our kids may seem fine. They go to school, laugh, and smile, and they understand how to function within our family community. It's been consistent all along. But if you listen closely, you'll hear them talk about their friends and other communities, revealing underlying issues. Friends can be unkind, even outright mean, and they are not meeting our child's needs. Our children feel confusion, frustration, loneliness, and anger. When the day's noise subsides, you can hear your child's concerns: "Why are my friends acting this way? Why are they mean and selfish?

Why is it challenging to make new friends? Why am I sad? Why do I feel so alone?"

Everyone is feeling the effects of the past three years. Our children are confused, stressed, and struggling to adapt to social situations. They're overwhelmed. My whole family is overwhelmed. I see it in my students, their choices, and the similarities among different groups. Our children are broken, but they're also resilient and eager to bridge the gaps in their social and cognitive development. Unfortunately, screens have sometimes filled in these gaps, replacing playground rules with social media norms. They believe that being outrageous gets likes and that meanness can make them go viral, and they apply these beliefs to their new communities.

One of the most challenging aspects of dealing with large groups, whether in teaching or parenting, is managing transitions. As parents, we can relate to this. Everything can be fine within the house, but as soon as it's time to load up the car and go somewhere, things can go awry. We discuss loading up the car, make lists, assign tasks, and yet, we often forget things – from simple items like shoes and water bottles to important ones like keys or wallets.

Transitions in the classroom represent a period of change. Expectations, rules, structure, and goals may all change, and students can seize this opportunity to create their own rules. Clear structure and explicit expectations during transitions are essential to prevent chaos. This principle applies to parenting too. As our kids transition between friends, family, and babysitters, the rules and routines should be evident. It's okay if the rules and routines differ; our kids just need to understand the expectations. Over the past three years, our lives have seen constant change, with rules and expectations often blurred by fear, anger, frustration, and uncertainty. The entire world experienced something new together – how to navigate a deadly pandemic. Let's take a closer look at the major changes of the past three years:

School Timeline:
1. My school district closed schools on March 16, 2020.
2. On March 30th, we transitioned to continuity of learning, with no new instruction.
3. In August 2020, virtual teaching with new instruction commenced.
4. By February 2021, we adopted a hybrid/concurrent teaching model.
5. In August 2021, we returned to school with masks and social distancing measures in place.
6. On February 24th, 2022, the mask mandate in schools was lifted.
7. On March 1st, the mask mandate on buses was also lifted.
8. Finally, in August 2022, we returned to a "normal" school setting.

This period marked two years and seven months of constant change before we could return to a sense of normalcy. Eight major transitions, and countless minor ones.

Cognitive and Social Development:

1. We lost every community except for our family for the initial two weeks.
2. We experienced isolation and social distancing for nearly a year.
3. Masks, which blocked facial expressions, were a part of our lives for almost two years.
4. Our exposure to peers and adults was limited for nearly two years.
5. We lost access to sports and school-based clubs for eight months.
6. We missed direct in-person instruction for almost seventeen months.

Media, News, and Global Events:

1. The initial shutdown due to the virus was a major global event.
2. Initially, there were conflicting beliefs about the virus's impact, with some believing it only affected older individuals with major stressors, similar to the flu.
3. There was confusion over whether masks were necessary, required, or effective.
4. The origin of the virus was a subject of debate.
5. The 2020 election build-up and its aftermath were highly significant events.
6. "Tiger King" became a cultural phenomenon.
7. Social outrage erupted over civilian deaths.
8. The January 6th Capitol news was a major event.
9. Fake news and a loss of trust in media sources became prevalent.

10. The development and distribution of vaccines were pivotal in the ongoing pandemic response, but they were controversial

Over the past three years, we've weathered a storm of fear. This fear has, at times, boiled over into anger and frustration. I understand the frustration, anger, brokenness, and depression that many of us feel. I feel it. However, instead of coming together and working through these challenges, we often find ourselves drifting apart and demeaning those with differing ideas or viewpoints. Our kids witness, hear, and read about this divisive atmosphere, especially on social media platforms that use fancy math and algorithms to feed us content that keeps us glued to our screens.

The last three years have been difficult to process, and many of us are still engaged in ongoing arguments about various issues. The fallout continues to affect us. I know adults who have lost the ability to think critically and process the multitude of information and opinions out there. I've personally stopped seeking out or reading about these topics, and my daughters have grown weary of it. My wife can only digest these matters in small doses.

But how are our kids coping? It's a challenge because one of the best ways to navigate complex issues is through dialogue with people we respect. However, these topics often become defining elements of a person's identity, leading many to avoid even considering the other side or acknowledging the unintended consequences of their beliefs. Empathy for differing perspectives has given way to animosity, with those holding different opinions often being labeled as "morons" or "idiots." The worst part is the pervasive shouting and degradation of anyone with a dissenting viewpoint.

I grew up with the principle of "stop and think, weigh both sides, and make a good decision" ingrained in me. We were taught to think before we act, a lesson I can still hear my dad imparting. That seems to have been discarded, replaced by blind allegiance to our chosen leaders, with the opposition automatically branded as idiots.

Our kids are keen observers, and they absorb not only what we say but also what we do. Modeling the behavior we want to see in our children is one of the most effective ways to be good parents. I'm aware of this, and I strive to do it, but like many parents, I stumble as often as I succeed. Parenting is a relentless, lifelong endeavor. Demonstrating good behavior during easy times is straightforward; it's our actions during difficult moments that our children truly remember.

Part 2 - Social Media and Its Impact

Our leaders are in such a fervent pursuit of victory that they often disregard the methods they employ. Instead of relying on facts to persuade the public, they resort to name-calling, essentially using playground rules to win arguments. They seem to be engaging in a contest of calling each other liars, with the victor being whoever speaks last or the loudest. This behavior isn't limited to leaders but also extends to social media, where even ads employ scare tactics to keep us in a state of fear, making us easier to manipulate.

To be fair, my state leader appeared to be a strong leader during the pandemic, and I found myself agreeing with most of his decisions. My perspective isn't filtered through the lens of a political party; I've lost faith in both parties. Instead, I view things through a coaching lens – would I want this person as my head coach or in charge of my favorite hockey team? My state leader made commendable real-time decisions, and I was impressed with his leadership. However, he seemed to be the exception rather than the standard. In times of crisis, we need strong leaders, not immature, power-hungry, ego-driven ones.

The greatest coaches often emphasize, "When the team wins, it's the players' credit. When the team loses, it's the coach's fault." It appears that all our leaders have lost sight of the team. They are so preoccupied with retaining their positions that they've forgotten to consider what's best for the team.

Our students have had to grapple with all of this. Our children have witnessed family members arguing and shouting at each other. They've picked sides or been placed on one. Our children have survived, but they have been affected. I see the impact every day at work, and I see new students every two days. Over the past three years, I've worked with over 12,000 students from urban, suburban, and rural areas. Our children are socially, mentally, and emotionally affected. Some are more affected than others, but none remain untouched.

Social media plays a significant role in this. It's not that social media is inherently mean; rather we, the users, tend to gravitate towards mean content. I'm guilty of this too – I find humor in watching people stumble and fall. I enjoy seeing a person get their comeuppance, often giggling at their misfortune. My phone knows this about me and serves up more of the same content. I revel in watching train wrecks. Part of the reason for this may be my job, where I must maintain filters. Many filters. So, when I'm at home, with no need for restraint, I can simply laugh. No need for first aid, no pondering, "Did I warn them about that?" At work, I spring into action, grabbing the first aid kit and taking responsibility. On my phone, I'm just an observer, watching, laughing, reminiscing about my own mishaps, and moving on to the next reel. No responsibility, no cleanup. I can simply relish in the person's momentary lapse in judgment. But I'm older, and I've had my fair share of falls, broken bones, and injuries. I understand the real-life consequences.

I don't think all of our children fully grasp this. I say this because I see them treating each other as if they were watching content. If they dislike something or someone, they leave a vicious comment and swipe to the next reel. Our children have grown accustomed to being mean to each other, believing it's normal and acceptable. They see the likes that trolls get online and observe these videos going viral. They don't comprehend that real communities necessitate different rules. They don't understand the impact of their words and actions. It's time to reintroduce the "Golden Rule."

When we know we'll never encounter someone again, it's easy to be angry and mean. Think about driving – the car in front of you behaves in a way you dislike, and horns honk, gestures are made, and harsh words are exchanged. People may drive aggressively to demonstrate how much of an inconvenience the other driver is being. But we don't act this way in a real community. We can't berate and insult a cashier in our favorite grocery store or show them the finger if we don't like how they are behaving because we intend to return to the store. As much as we may want to vent our frustration on the clerk at our favorite fast-food restaurant, we also want our food and anticipate returning to the store.

This understanding keeps most of us in check. If we want to return, we must empathize with the clerk. Perhaps they're having a tough day, and our smile and kind words can lighten their burden. As adults who may have worked such jobs, we understand how challenging they can be, and we feel empathy because it's our store. I believe our children still think it's social media – scream, yell, get likes, go viral. They don't understand that they have to return to the group and their actions have ramifications.

Screens are the new drug. We are all addicted to our screens. They have been designed to stimulate our brain, releasing dopamine. Social media rewards us with likes and algorithms are designed to keep us clicking the screen. I am not a research scientist, I am not a psychologist, I am a teacher. But I don't allow my daughters to have social media on their phone. I am also not naive; I know that they still use it. It can be great, but it can also be horrible. Regarding social media use, HelpGuide.org states that "multiple studies have found a strong link between heavy social media and an increased risk for depression, anxiety, loneliness, self-harm, and even suicidal thoughts."

Social media is not a substitute teacher, it is not a babysitter, and it is not a parent. We need to manage our addictions to the screen so we can manage our kids' addiction to their screens.

Part 3 - Forgotten, Never Taught, or Toxic Stress

Remember how we placed our children in front of screens and told them to use those screens for learning? At first, it was for just a few hours, and then it became a whole school day. We didn't really provide proper training. We were so focused on adapting ourselves that we simply assumed the students would figure it out. From March 2020 to June 2020, our message was clear: "Get online, find your work, and complete it." There was no direct instruction, and we expected about 2 to 3 hours of online work. We didn't teach them how to effectively use computers for learning. We didn't differentiate between good and bad websites. There was no formal training.

Now, imagine the temptation this presented. They had a magical box that knew everything, filled with every imaginable video, song, and game. And they were supposed to be on the magic box but follow a teacher through a lesson that paled in comparison to everything else in that box. We gave them access to the social media substitute. It was an impossible task to have our kids navigate, right? I know I would have failed. I'd be playing a game in another window. I can't even sit through a meeting without fiddling with my phone because I'm addicted to it. Yet we expected children to do this without parental supervision.

I grew up without the internet, but I was trained in how to use it. I learned how to distinguish a good website from a bad one. I was told to stay off social media if I valued my job. I was instructed to keep everything private, and I was educated about the consequences of making poor choices on social media. I saw news articles that linked such choices to life-altering consequences. A significant portion of our children haven't received this training. Social media has changed the rules and expectations for users, and the race to become an influencer has altered our behaviors.

When we returned in the fall for virtual learning, the children spent the entire school day on the computer. When we came back with masks, class size was smaller, and a lot of students were still virtual. Then we all came back with masks, and we thought everything was behind us.

I believe we placed an expectation on them to remember all the crucial rules, but our children either forgot them or, perhaps, were never properly taught them in the first place. Even on the best days, students struggle to remember what happened the week before. The "summer slide" is a real phenomenon, which is why some school districts have moved to year-round schooling. Our children can't keep up with all the expectations because we've changed them too many times. They can't even remember the rules. While older children might have received more instruction and remembered most of the rules, some forgetting and confusion is still unavoidable.

I sat down and tried to recall what happened during the pandemic, but I couldn't. I couldn't remember details, timelines, or important activities. I had a vague sense of major events and when they occurred, but I had to sift through emails, newspaper headlines, and my wife's Facebook to piece everything together. I interviewed both my daughters, and they struggled to remember everything too. It's difficult to remember everything during stressful events because your mind is in survival mode, allocating resources that would otherwise be used for memory towards survival.

Our children have forgotten all the playground rules. They've lost the ability to behave appropriately in social settings and large groups. I've seen them shout things in my class as if they were at a football game, but what they're shouting isn't socially acceptable, and it seems like they don't understand that. They've been uncharacteristically mean and hurtful to each other, and it appears they don't grasp how hurtful they're being. They also don't comprehend the lasting impact of a single mean sentence. I've always heard that it takes ten positive comments to outweigh the impact of one negative comment.

Our kids need to relearn how to read facial expressions and understand that they'll encounter their peers again tomorrow. This isn't social media where you never have to see that person again. In our learning and social communities, we can't block or hide contacts. When we interact with real people in our community and are mean, we damage those relationships for a long time. Our kids don't realize this.

Our children are experiencing stress, and so are parents and adults. When I looked up the definition of stress, I found the World Health Organization's definition:

> Stress is a state of worry or mental tension caused by a difficult situation. Stress is a natural human response that prompts us to address challenges and threats in our lives. Everyone experiences stress to some degree. The way we respond to stress, however, makes a big difference to our overall well-being.

A little bit of stress can be a positive thing. It helps us navigate everyday challenges. I personally worry about challenging situations and get nervous before big events or tasks. This nervousness prompts me to constantly think about the task at hand, running different scenarios in my head. This preparation helps me be successful when it's time to tackle the task. I like to call this approach "moving with purpose." I identify the desired outcome, think about the best way to achieve it, and then take action. It's something we should all strive for. We all need to move with purpose.

Acute stress typically triggers our fight, flight, freeze, or appease response. However, it's important to remember that this is acute stress, an immediate response. This is why we plan for the worst and hope for the best. Organizations like the Red Cross and coaching programs are excellent at teaching this approach. Being able to consider stressful scenarios before we find ourselves in them helps reduce our fight, flight, freeze, or appease response and enables us to take purposeful action toward achieving our goals.

Chronic, long-term stress, on the other hand, can infiltrate all our body's major systems and disrupt our internal balance, or homeostasis. Chronic stress is particularly challenging because it's always present and unrelenting.

COVID-19 is an unprecedented and unknown threat, and it brings with it a great deal of stress. The last major pandemic to affect the United States was the Spanish flu of 1918. To have experienced it, you'd need to be around 105 years old, and perhaps 108-110 to remember it. The world is grappling with a deadly global pandemic for the first time in most of our lives. No one knows for certain what will happen, so we have to prepare for the worst while hoping for the best. The virus doesn't take a day off. It doesn't care about our beliefs. It's simply a bundle of proteins and nucleic acids waiting for the opportunity to hijack your cells and turn them into virus-producing factories. The virus is a source of chronic stress.

The pandemic has been all-encompassing, and we've essentially been constructing the bridge as we attempt to cross it. Stress has permeated every aspect of our lives—our families, communities, workplaces, sports, churches—there's been no escape from the pandemic-induced stress.

With social-emotional stressors, our natural response to "tend or befriend" usually kicks in. We want to help heal others' wounds, lift them when they fall, and find solace in shared experiences with friends. However, COVID-19 isolated us from each other, disrupting these crucial coping mechanisms. Many of us now feel anxious about gathering in large groups or attending social events to build and strengthen friendships.

To cope with this toxic stress, we must adopt a deliberate approach. We have to move with purpose. Coping mechanisms need to become intentional habits. Exercise, healthy eating, meditation, strong communities, adequate sleep, and reducing exposure to external stressors, such as smartphones, TV, and excessive news consumption, all need to become core values. Therapy, forming supportive friend groups, and engaging in honest conversations should become part of our regular routine. By taking care of ourselves, we'll be better equipped to care for our children.

It's not easy. We all struggle to consistently adhere to these habits, but we work towards them. My wife and I are actively teaching our daughters the importance of these stress-reducing habits. It's an ongoing dance, where we sometimes take steps forward and other times step backward or even tread on each other's toes. But that's life, and that's what makes it so enjoyable. With the right dance partner, everything feels right, and when we stumble or fall, it's an opportunity to reflect, refocus, and try again.

Our children have experienced an extraordinary three years filled with confusion, missed developmental opportunities, and the loss of once-in-a-lifetime events. Nevertheless, they remain amazing. In the 2022-2023 school year, I noticed more than ever before students seeking my attention and engaging in wonderful conversations. They know how to converse with adults one-on-one, likely due to the lessons taught by their parents over the past three years. We lost nearly all our communities, except for our families, which became our one constant. Maybe I am crazy, maybe I just value a good conversation differently, but these small side conversations have really stuck with me.

Throughout the pandemic, our family had to compensate for nearly everything we lost. Social media and the news helped fill the gaps that family alone couldn't. It's clear to me that the willingness of so many students to engage in conversation is a testament to the strength of the family. It appears that, before the pandemic, students were often focused solely on their peers and rarely sought out conversations with adults. However, in the 2022-2023 school year, they seemed comfortable engaging in meaningful discussions, actively seeking out adults rather than their peers. Perhaps this is a flight response, as interacting with peers may have become so stressful that they avoid it.

Empathy, the ability to understand someone else's thoughts and feelings in a given situation, can be challenging to muster when we're stressed, upset, afraid, angry, or feeling hopeless. Yet empathy is needed now more than ever. Consider your playground, your safe space, your best or worst childhood moments, and then think about what our children have missed in those three years. We have the power to help our kids heal and recover, but it must start with empathy. Once we can truly put ourselves in our children's shoes, we can guide them forward. Their stressors are unique to their generation, and by understanding them, we can help our children navigate the toxic stress they carry and surround themselves with. Let's move with purpose to instill healthy habits of the mind and body in our children.

Chapter 8
Time to Reflect So We Can Move Forward with Purpose.

If we use the metaphor of the pandemic as a forest, it feels like we're currently standing within the woods, with a glimpse of the clearing just beyond our reach. While we're not entirely out of the woods, we can at least see the edge. There are still potential hazards ahead, and we'll need to navigate them, but I'm optimistic that this leg of our journey will be less challenging. It's not yet time for celebration, but it's crucial to reflect on our accomplishments, acknowledge our losses, and chart our path forward.

In the same way, it's essential to recognize that our children have also been profoundly affected by the pandemic. They may be grappling with their own issues, yet they might not fully understand what's troubling them, or they might not realize that we are genuinely interested in knowing. As a result, they might feel isolated and without a confidant they can trust.

Our students and kids remain remarkable individuals to connect with. They possess wonderful personalities, boundless enthusiasm, unique perspectives, and aspirations that are truly contagious. These positive qualities persist despite the colossal cosmic curveball life has thrown our way, and we've all had to contend with it in our own manner. Some of us excelled, while others merely watched the pitch go by, but each one of us found ourselves in the batter's box and had to face that cosmic curveball.

For me, I feel like the kid who inadvertently fouled the cosmic curveball into the neighbor's window. Now is the time for us to review the game tape, contemplate how we managed that unexpected pitch, and strategize how we want to confront the rest of the game.

It's of paramount importance to reflect, evaluating both the favorable and unfavorable aspects of our journey, as well as considering our future. We need to think about how we can move forward.

Not long ago, my family watched a stand-up comedy special on Netflix, *Hannah Gadsby: Nanette*. Hannah Gadsby shares a lengthy and humorous story about an event in her life. For years she had stopped right at the funny point, and everyone laughed. Everyone except her. She knew the truth, but instead of processing it, she hid it behind humor. In this special she completes the story. She revealed the painful truth behind it. The genuine narrative was heartbreaking, but she felt compelled to share it. She had perpetuated the lie for so long that she couldn't move forward. She explained that embracing the truth was the only way for her to heal.

We are in a similar situation. We are still hurting, confused, and wondering why we are not our pre-pandemic selves. I think it is because we are broken on the inside. We need to take the time to figure out ourselves so we can move forward. Now is the time to reflect.

Part 1 - Let's Reflect

We've made it through this challenging time, and it's important to take a moment to reflect. I hope you have found reasons to be grateful. I hope you've identified areas you'd like to change and have started planning for your future. Let's celebrate our victories, no matter how big or small, and address the challenges ahead.

Consider your children's accomplishments; perhaps just getting online was a significant achievement for them. Maybe their determination to access the internet was their personal triumph. Joining a team or experiencing a sleepover could have been their wins. Victories can be as simple as taking a small step or as major as achieving a long-term goal; they can encompass everything in between.

Small victories can occur daily. If you're struggling to recognize these small wins, keep it straightforward. Embrace the philosophy of Dory in *Finding Nemo* – "Just keep swimming! (32:15-32:42)" Waking up every day and striving to navigate through life's challenges is a major accomplishment. Successfully managing virtual teaching is a monumental achievement. Returning to school, reengaging in sports, rejoining clubs, and reconnecting with communities that may have been lost in those initial weeks of the pandemic are significant wins. Coping with family members who fell ill is another testament to your strength. Discovering the joys of the library, enjoying a family show, or engaging in meaningful conversations – these are all substantial wins. Over the past three years, I've had the privilege of teaching over 12,000 students, and as parents, you have done an exceptional job. I love hearing about all the things they have done and what they value.

For me, I find solace in putting my thoughts down on paper. If you're struggling to identify those small wins, consider journaling; it can be more than just writing. Incorporate images, drawings, colors, paintings, sculptures, or even create jewelry or bake something. Find your creative genius and express yourself.

Engaging in conversations with your family can also be a powerful way to reflect. Use simple questions that invite complex answers:

- "What was the best part of the pandemic?"
- "Can you share your fondest memory from virtual school?"
- "What do you miss the most now that the pandemic is no longer a hot topic?"
- "Aside from family, what was your lifeline during the pandemic?"
- "If you knew another pandemic was coming next year, how would you prepare?"

- "If you could go back in time and give advice to your pre-pandemic self, what would you say?"

I'm always amazed at the insights my daughters and students share. Your smartphone can be a valuable tool in triggering positive memories. Look through your favorite photos or review your calendar. For those inclined, scrapbooking can be a wonderful family project. There is no one-size-fits-all method for reflection; discover your family values and use them as your guide. I'm certain you'll be pleasantly surprised, just as I have been.

Teachers, coaches, parents – we all engage in reflection. Celebrating the good is often a straightforward task, while addressing the bad can prove to be more challenging, particularly for my generation – Gen X. I belong to a generation raised by Baby Boomer parents, and my grandparents lived through World War II. The values instilled in us were rooted in hard work and resilience. We were expected to be tough and unwavering, just like them. Displaying emotions or admitting to weaknesses was discouraged. Failure was often met with harsh criticism, whether from our parents or our peers, and we learned to conceal our vulnerabilities. Breaking down the emotional walls we built was not easy.

With that said, I'm also a problem solver. I had trouble learning to read and write in school. School presented its challenges, and I was consistently reminded that I was the least academically inclined in my family. In my youth, this was a source of pain, and I had to bury it, as my brothers would exploit it. Over time, this pain transformed into anger and eventually into determination. To succeed, I knew I had to work harder, smarter, and differently. This perspective helped me navigate my academic failures – I could identify the problem, but I didn't dwell on it; instead, I focused on finding a solution.

The bad was bad, but the acknowledgment of the bad is crucial. It's akin to recognizing regret in golfers. They want another chance at the same hole. They ask for a "Mulligan," another shot. Gamers will also replay levels. What would you do differently? Remember, you're not alone; we've all had our share of setbacks. Contemplating the situation, how you handled it, and how you can improve is a vital aspect of learning and growth. Some may find it easy, while others might engage in negative self-talk. However, the difference lies in perspective. Embracing the bad allows us to assess our actions and plan for improvement, empowering us rather than breaking us down. Negative self-talkers, on the other hand, approach mistakes with self-condemnation, hindering personal growth.

When reflecting on the bad, maintain an optimistic outlook. None of us had experienced a pandemic before; we were all learning as we went along. Identifying the challenges and considering how to address them is how we shape the future.

I believe that reflecting on the things you want to change is essential for setting meaningful goals. Personally, I've always referred to my goals as "dreams," a term that fills me with excitement and happiness. I have an abundance of dreams, quite possibly numbering in the millions. Setting and pursuing goals has always been a strength of mine; they serve as a source of nourishment for my soul, igniting my motivation simply by having them in mind. I take great pleasure in contemplating the myriad possibilities, even if I don't manage to accomplish all of them. Some remain dreams, and that's perfectly fine because thinking about them brings me joy. Here's how I go about it.

I categorize my dreams into three main areas: those for today, those for the current season, and those for the next couple of years. Short-term goals are the ones I can achieve in a day or maybe within a week. Long-term goals are focused on the season, spanning the next few months or the year. Then there are the big, hairy goals, the ones that might take five or ten years to achieve.

Small goals, the ones I can accomplish daily, help me feel successful every day and keep me on the right track. They contribute to my sense of achievement, boosting my self-esteem. Lately, though, these small goals have become increasingly challenging to complete. Simple tasks like going to bed on time, waking up as planned, folding laundry, or finishing a project have started to feel like daunting challenges. Dinner, in particular, has become a real struggle. It's surprising how much stress planning and preparing a meal has brought into my life. It's a relentless task that is still overwhelming to me, and I can't help but chuckle at the absurdity of it all. I acknowledge that I need to work on changing the stress associated with this daily chore.

Medium goals, on the other hand, provide the "why" behind my actions. They help answer the question of whether something is worth it. These goals are the things that truly make me happy; they are about creating, experiencing, and feeling specific moments. It could be a trip, a hobby, or a health goal that motivates me to tackle the smaller tasks. These medium goals are the silver linings that make the less enjoyable moments worthwhile. I have trips I dream of all the time: the Smoky Mountains, Iceland, Greece, Utah, Scotland, England, Spain, Africa, Antarctica, I want to see everything. I also have a hobby; I flint knap. I love to make arrowheads and knife blades out of rock and glass. Finding time to create neolithic tools and talking to friends that love to do the same is awesome. I also want to be the best ice hockey coach and player I can be. I constantly think about how to be in better shape and how to teach my skaters.

The big goals are the ones that stand out. They represent significant accomplishments that are sometimes referred to as "bucket list" items. However, I personally don't favor this term for a specific reason. Many people believe they will live for a very long time. This idea gives them a timeline that allows them to push back their dreams. But therein lies the issue – goals need a defined timeline to motivate us to work towards them. We need that sense of urgency to drive us to accomplish them.

When it comes to our children, most of the big goals are often imposed on them. They're encouraged to graduate from high school, acquire the skills to drive, find a good job (or any job), learn a trade or attend college, and strive for success. In their case, short-term and long-term goals are tremendously important, even if these big goals are typically set by others. Unfortunately, we don't always involve our children in the process of setting and pursuing these goals, and it's a skill we should be teaching them.

As parents, if we can establish our short and long-term goals, we can also guide our children in doing the same. Goals for us parents, goals for the family, and goals for our children – they're all valuable. Hopefully, there's a dreamer or a goal-setter within your family. However, if not, you can teach your child how to embark on this journey. Start with simplicity, beginning with significant daily accomplishments such as chores, maintaining a clean room, doing the dishes, preparing breakfast, adhering to wake-up and bedtime schedules, managing screen and TV time, making smart food choices, planning meals, and participating in sports and clubs. At the end of the day, take a moment to reflect. Making connections between the goals, your feelings, and your ability to do the activities that feed your soul will help you value the process. When we can see the benefit, it becomes easier to set goals again and again.

In my family, dinner serves as our time to come together. We try to dine together and plan for the upcoming day. We discuss the events of the day and, if time permits, plan for the week ahead. We also aim to clean up the house together, making it a shared goal. It's not something we consistently achieve, but when we do, it's a magical moment. This evening gathering signifies the close of the day; we talk about what happened and what we did, then we plan for tomorrow. Being able to rely on each other helps to strengthen our family bonds. Each member has a voice and the opportunity to seek assistance or share ideas. This family time is akin to our community meeting, and it holds great importance for all of us, particularly for my wife and my youngest daughter.

We recognize the challenges or shortcomings we faced in order to set our sights on future goals. It requires an honest effort, using setbacks to change habits, improve recurring situations, and enhance our community, rather than using them to shame or degrade any family member. Growth necessitates honesty and support, alongside patience and understanding. These goals are often complex, intertwined with other aspects of life. As we change one thing, it can have a ripple effect on others. Be patient, be adaptable, set your goals, and don't hesitate to adjust them. Sometimes they may feel too easy or too difficult, but we all aspire to be in the Goldilocks zone with our goals – just right to keep us motivated, challenged, and successful.

Part 2 - My Battle with My Inner Demons

When I reflect on the past three years, it often feels like a blur, requiring deliberate effort to recollect. Seriously, there is a hole in my memory. The good things seemed to evade me; there are stolen moments. They were not part of a large plan, so they seem disconnected, disorganized and hard to remember. It is like I was digging random holes in the backyard. This hole gave me family time, the next hole gave me a dog, this hole over here gave me time for flint knapping. Because I had these moments and filled them randomly, I have trouble feeling the accomplishment.

It's taken me most of the summer of 2023 to remember the things that happened during the pandemic. When I dig through my memories and find a win, I am thankful, I smile, and I see the value it added to our family. As I've recalled more and more from that dark time, I've realized that my family has numerous reasons to be thankful.

I am grateful for the increased family time we've had. Our new dog has also brought immeasurable joy to our lives. During the challenges of virtual school, my coworkers and I managed to make the best out of a challenging situation; after being given lemons, we managed to make lemonade. My hobbies have become a source of solace, and witnessing my family coming together to grow stronger and more resilient has been heartwarming. I am thankful for the conversations I've had and the friends who've provided support. My involvement in ice hockey, both playing and coaching, has been a source of fulfillment. I've also had the privilege of spending quality time with world-class mentors, and our family had the opportunity to travel. I'm thankful that I still have a job. In many ways, we've had significant victories.

My daughters, in their own unique way, embraced the pandemic in ways only young people can. We became a tighter-knit family unit, and they adapted to the challenges of remote learning, navigating the loss of tangible friendships and watching their friends become reduced to the tiny circle icons online. They faced the challenges posed by glitches and the diverse teaching styles of their educators. They even learned how to train our dog. They encountered friendship dynamics, worked through hurt feelings, and embraced new social groups and communities. I hope they've discovered newfound strengths and can take pride in the new skills they've acquired.

My wife played a crucial role in saving our family during this trying time. She made the difficult decision to leave her job and focused on our daughters and me. She worked through her own stresses, found a new job that she enjoys, and devoted time to volunteer and support our daughters' school activities. She began focusing on her physical health and became the driving force behind our family's goal setting. She tackled the seemingly minor things that we had collectively pushed aside as unimportant, and I couldn't be more grateful.

Despite our achievements, it's essential to remember that numerous wins don't equate to an absence of challenges. Stress and failures often lurk between the moments of triumph, and this is the aspect that I'm currently grappling with. If we've had so many significant victories, why do I still feel bad? I feel yucky, like I have a spot of rot that I cannot get rid of. Why do I feel this way? The straightforward answer is that the stress hasn't dissipated. To change our future and lift ourselves out of this emotional slump, we must confront the challenges we've encountered. Just like the comedian that embraced her pain and shared it, we have to embrace our pain and work through it.

I, along with my family, have experienced various hardships during the pandemic. Hundreds of little disappointments and failures, building up like mosquito bites. One is frustrating, three is bad, now imagine your whole body covered with tiny bites driving you nuts. That is what we are all dealing with.

I found myself battling depression as the pandemic unfolded. I know that the circumstances that caused my depression were out of my control, but I wish I would have addressed it sooner. It's something I'm working diligently to change. When I think about how I dealt with this challenge, I totally want a Mulligan. Worries about my family's well-being led me to neglect my own health. I ceased working out, turned to stress eating, and indulged in unhealthy snacks for momentary comfort. My shopping cart filled with cookies and Little Debbie snacks, and ice cream became a staple in my diet. I gained 15 pounds, and I was pushing myself to the limit, struggling to make it through each week.

My family also faced emotional struggles. We faced significant losses, with my mom and father-in-law passing away. My daughters grappled with feelings of sadness and loneliness, and my wife's stress became so overwhelming that she had to leave her job. Both of my daughters and my wife had evenings when everything was just too much, and they were in tears. There were deep feelings and deep sadness that surfaced when the world slowed down. You feel helpless holding your daughter as she cries, not knowing why she is upset or if you can help her.

Our long-anticipated fifteenth wedding anniversary trip never came to fruition. This really crushed me mentally. The plan was a long time in the making, and I was excited to share the adventure with my wife. I was excited for quality time to reconnect without the distractions of everyday life, a vacation without our kids, so we could focus on each other.

We had dreams to travel to Greece for our honeymoon back in 2005, but we let the travel agent talk us out of it. Then my older brother went with his daughter and had an amazing time. That lit the fire and I wanted to go. My wife was in, it was time to fix that old mistake we made. It is exciting to right a wrong, fix a problem, or just discover something new and this trip was going to be it.

The planning was done, we filled the days with exciting activities, hotels were picked, dates were set. All we had to do was pay for the trip and it was a done deal. In hindsight, I guess we were lucky. I was busy and dragging my feet on making the first payment. It was due on March 20th, 2020. Then school shut down, and our trip vanished into thin air. It could have been worse; I could have made that payment. Nonetheless, losing that trip hurt. It was a mental kick in the shins. I did not lose any money, just an experience. Still, losing the opportunity damaged my spirit for longer than I would like to admit.

I found myself caught in a cycle of depression and self-blame. The multitude of small wins we achieved made me feel as though I had no reason to be depressed. However, the crushing weight of dreams left unfulfilled was difficult to bear. I couldn't address any of this while consumed by anger and disappointment. My frustration with myself was merely a way to focus on the problem or, more accurately, to ignore it.

As the problem grew too significant to ignore, I reached a point of being a "hot mess." Yes, that should be a medical term. It means that you can barely get dressed and showered, and when you finally do, you want to call it a day. It means that you feel like the black cloud that is always in your mind is a comfortable type of pain that you enjoy, and you cannot fathom life without it. Focusing on the problem, focusing on the bad, is like being mentally stuck in the muck. It is important to identify the problem, but we cannot stop and focus on the bad. It was clear that I needed to shift my focus and concentrate on the solution.

Depression is a super villain, sapping one's vitality and making every aspect of life feel like an uphill battle. For me, work was my primary focus during this challenging period. As everything around us was in a state of flux, everyone was trying to find solutions. Keep in mind, when we started continuation of learning, we did not know if we were going to get paid. Our plan had not been approved by the state, we just knew that our students needed something. We had no idea what the state was going to approve, but we did it anyway. We had to trust the powers that be to do the right thing.

In my school district, it felt like an all-hands-on-deck situation, where every possible option was considered as we adapted to the changing circumstances. I couldn't help but feel like my job was on the chopping block. We are a program that runs outdoor education. We give students experiential learning. The easiest way to think about this is a field trip, but we are so much more than a field trip. We are exploring our county with our students. We are tour guides that teach, engage, and challenge our students as we explore our local parks and resources.

When we went virtual, no one was going on a field trip. It was clear that we couldn't continue with business as usual during this time of remote learning. My fear was that they would repurpose our team and that our program would be lost forever. The anxiety was overwhelming.

Looking back, I'm not certain that our program was ever truly at risk. However, when everything is rapidly evolving, it's natural to have doubts. While I trusted my boss and his immediate supervisors, I'd also seen administrators make sweeping decisions without considering the unintended consequences. So, there was a lingering sense of apprehension. I wanted our program to be so invaluable to the teachers and students that it would be irreplaceable. My boss shared this vision, but despite these ambitions, fear loomed over me every day.

Transitioning from spending my days outdoors to being tethered to a computer for the entire day was mentally draining. It was a crushing experience that left me emotionally exhausted. During of all these changes, I was also trying to support my family, particularly my mom. Unfortunately, my own well-being fell by the wayside.

Depression can feel like a weakness, and it's challenging to admit. I come from a generation where the idea of boys expressing their feelings was discouraged, but I'm learning to embrace a more open approach. My wife has been a driving force in challenging me to be more expressive, and I've made efforts in that direction. It genuinely helps when I do open up.

I understood that I was dealing with depression, and I hated it. I tried to set aside time for myself, but it always ended up as the last thing on my priority list. One escape I discovered was ice hockey. I joined a group of friends who rented ice time for pickup games once a week. While most other activities were on hold, we were able to continue due to the availability of the rink. I spent about 1 hour and 20 minutes on the ice each week, plus some social time afterward. In the context of a week with 168 hours, I was dedicating only about 4 hours to myself, and this came at the expense of sleep. It still wasn't enough.

Now, I know that I stole other times for myself. My phone was also a distraction. My hobbies were a safe place. But being at home is not the same. While in the house on the phone or playing in the garage, I was still dealing with things at home; I was on call. Being at the rink, I was inaccessible to my family. I could scream and yell, I could skate as fast as possible. I could push my physical limits and experience the moment. I forgot the world while I was on the ice. I was living in the moment. No pandemic, just the next pass, the next shot, the next goal. Just me and my friends trying to beat the other team. Just me and my team trying to win the Stanley Cup!

I think it was the not knowing that crushed my spirit. Not knowing when this was going to end. Not knowing if my job was going to exist next week. Not knowing if we were going to get sick. Not knowing if our loved ones were going to die. Not knowing what the future was going to look like. How can you have meaningful, attainable dreams if you don't know what tomorrow will look like? We set goals based on present conditions. If tomorrow looks like today, I want to do this. With the pandemic, the rules and expectations were constantly changing across the globe.

We did have the 1918 flu pandemic, which lasted five years. Using this as a loose guide was a blessing and a curse. It helped me believe that things would get better, but placing things on hold for five years was not an option for me. It broke me mentally. I was thinking of the problem. No, I was living the problem. Every morning I woke up to the problem. It was like the movie *Groundhog Day*. Stuck in a relentless cycle of not knowing when this is going to end. I had to relive the first day of school again and again. All of my students would change but they all had the same issues. Dealing with the same inappropriate behaviors day after day was mentally and physically exhausting.

The frequent change to our teaching structure was overwhelming. Rules were altered overnight, often without warning. My greatest fear was that my program would be canceled – have I mentioned that yet? I was also bitter about missing that anniversary trip we had eagerly planned for over a year.

Yet, I still had a job, I was still receiving a paycheck, and my wife and daughters were physically healthy. In the beginning of the pandemic, flying seemed impossible, but we were still able to travel locally, exploring nearby parks and states. I felt I had no reason to be upset, and I was mad at myself for feeling so depressed. It took a while to shift my focus toward the solution, taking baby steps in that direction.

Talking to my friends about my feelings and sharing my depression with my doctor proved to be helpful. They offered to connect me with a therapist, but I was initially reluctant. I understood why I was feeling this way, but I was stuck in a rut. I believed I could change it if I found the time, but it wasn't a priority. Conversations with friends made a significant difference; knowing that I wasn't alone in this struggle helped. I just needed something to ignite my motivation.

My wife observed this journey from an external standpoint and provided unwavering support. She is who encouraged me to make the trip to New Mexico to find some much-needed "me time" in October 2020. I traveled to New Mexico to meet up with my older brother. He has been my adventure buddy for the last three decades. My wife and family too, but they move at a different pace. My brother and I are of the same mind and travel with the same goal: "let's do everything, we can sleep when we get home."

He kind of took over my dad's role as my companion on adventures. It happened organically. My mom and dad got a divorce, so they disappeared for a time, and my brothers and I rallied around each other. My younger brother had a serious girlfriend, and I was working in California. As brothers, we were drifting apart, going our own ways. My older brother's friend got me a job teaching at our former high school, and when I called my brother to tell him I was going to explore California for a week before coming home, he said he would pick me up at camp and come with me. We explored Yosemite National Park and snorkeled in the kelp forests off the coast of Monterey Bay. It was a truly life changing trip. And that was that. We were adventure buddies for life.

After meeting my brother in New Mexico, we hiked Mt. Wheeler, explored Ourey and Telluride. We conquered both via ferratas on the same day. A via ferrata is a trail on the cliff face made of iron rungs and ladders. The trip was the mental floss I needed. We pushed ourselves hard and the stress of the pandemic was forgotten. But the stress was still there, just hidden for the week.

When I got back to work, the stress returned along with the "not knowing." Around this time, everyone was showing stress and teachers became targets again. Friends and families were venting and the issues with school were labeled the teachers' fault. Along with all the stress of teaching online, we became targets for every policy decision that was made. I am a teacher. I do what the state and district boards of education dictate. I do respond to our union's

202

questions, and I give my opinions when asked, but our board of education makes the policies. Being the trash can for everyone's frustration sucks, especially since I am powerless to do anything about it.

When I got back from New Mexico, more and more friends were starting to travel, and my wife started pushing for a family trip. We have made this a priority in our family. We travel. We sacrifice nice cars, eating out, and bedroom furniture to save for trips. We still have a lot of furniture from our childhood; I would rather travel than get a new bedroom set. I would rather travel than have the top-of-the-line car. I would rather travel than eat out several times a week. Travel has been a priority.

By the time we embarked on our trip to Zion it was the summer of 2022, and my body had reached its breaking point. I was plagued by foot and hip issues, and pain had become a daily companion. Sleep was elusive, and I found myself relying on ibuprofen just to catch a few hours of rest. I was furious with my body for betraying me, and that anger finally became a catalyst for change. When I returned from Zion, I initiated physical therapy to address my physical ailments. While it did provide some relief, I must admit I was a less-than-stellar patient. I often neglected my physical therapy homework. I had let myself go for too long, I had lost my good habits. The stress had seeped into major body systems. I am still trying to heal.

Stress is a formidable opponent; it accumulates, lurks in the shadows, and slowly erodes your well-being. Managing it is a daily chore. Neglecting it, as I did for too long, only allows it to fester. Effective stress management involves establishing daily priorities and habitual actions such as exercise, laughter, personal rewards, small achievements, proper hydration, healthier eating, quality family time, maintaining a clean environment, sticking to a structured routine, and learning to say "no." I know this, but I had to make these concepts a priority. I needed to move with purpose.

Going into the 2022-2023 school year I was heading in the right direction. Physical therapy, working out more, back to in-person instruction. I had no idea that this was going to be the hardest year of teaching ever. The students had forgotten everything. Expectations were not realistic, and I was so excited to be working with real students again that I did not stop to reflect on what they would really need. I don't think many people did. We just expected everyone to magically go back to our pre-pandemic life flawlessly. Wow, what a shock! Surviving that school year was tough. Getting to the summer of 2023 was an exercise in perseverance. I seriously wanted to quit in February. I have what I believe to be the greatest job in the whole school system, and I wanted to quit. I can only imagine what the other teachers felt.

The summer of 2023 felt like the first time I could truly breathe since March 13th, 2020. It was a season to focus on myself, placing my needs first and everything else coming second. The journey to reach this point had seemed insurmountable. I'd been eagerly awaiting summer since February, and the journey had felt like a crawl to June on my hands and knees. Making it through each workday had been a monumental effort, and my mental faculties were drained. My capacity to make decisions outside of work was nearly extinguished.

Once the summer arrived, it became a time for setting personal goals, playing, and taking a closer look at my family's needs while making necessary adjustments. I had aspirations to organize the rocks in my garage and the room in the basement that harbored more rocks. I am a flint knapper that lives on the east coast of the United States. We don't have access to high quality rocks to work with, so I have been collecting material. I have lots of rocks, mostly obsidian. Exploring our local river, crafting knives, and improving my skills in ice hockey and flint knapping were all on my summer to-do list, and I was brimming with excitement.

However, my excitement didn't necessarily translate to my family. They were navigating their own stress, having lost friends and their familiar routines. I had been so preoccupied with my own pursuits that I failed to fully appreciate their stress. My attempts to engage my daughters were often met with failure. When I asked them what they wanted to do, "nothing" was the go-to response. I attempted more direct questions like, "Anyone want to go to the store with me?" to no avail. Eventually I stopped asking. My wife took the initiative to create a list of fun activities, which she posted on the refrigerator. Unfortunately, it got buried under other things, and for a while, we found ourselves drifting aimlessly as a family.

While my wife was working, she was deeply concerned about our family. She wanted us to establish a routine to bring some stability back into our lives. I resisted the idea, craving more free time, and my daughters shared my reluctance. However, my wife and I recognized that our daughters needed structure, not unstructured free time. They needed friends, hobbies, and activities to help them regain skills and experiences that had been lost during the pandemic. We also felt it was essential for them to have responsibilities.

To address this, we began using the time immediately after dinner to work together on cleaning up the house. It was effective, but on busier days, sticking to the plan became more challenging. So, we eventually assigned specific chores and set deadlines for their completion. This approach worked well if we gave the occasional reminder.

My oldest daughter is in the tenth grade. She's fiercely independent but also quite sensitive, carrying a fair amount of emotional baggage. She loves to engage in conversations when the timing is right, but she can be quite guarded when the moment is wrong. Free time and chores were not her preferred activities. To keep her engaged, I enrolled her in skating lessons, and she began rollerblading regularly. Her friends also wanted to spend time with her, which served as an incentive for her to complete chores. Although she still had her challenging days, she seemed to be adapting to the summer routine, and my wife and I were gradually understanding her better.

My youngest daughter is in eighth grade, and she presented different challenges. She often appeared content spending time in her room playing Minecraft. When we restricted her screen time, she turned to reading books, showing a preference for alone time. While we attempted scheduling hangouts with her peers, her friends had busy schedules during the summer, making it difficult to coordinate. Nevertheless, we signed her up for field hockey, hoping this would be a good choice for her in high school. The only downside was that her practice sessions were on Sunday and Wednesday nights, which still left her with limited opportunities to interact with friends. However, two of her friends also joined field hockey, and she appeared to enjoy it, which was a win for us as parents.

Fortunately, her summer birthday presented an opportunity for her to engage in a long-term project with a timeline, encompassing small, intermediate, and significant goals. Her birthday party was a Barbie-themed sleepover with four of her friends. Planning her birthday party became an exciting venture. She created a wish list and hunted for everything pink in the house. The planning involved organizing meals, creating decorations, cleaning, texting and coordinating with friends. It involved a scavenger hunt of photos from each year of her life, and her older sister even joined in the fun.

The party went well, offering a glimpse into the dynamics of a group of five young teenagers. Odd numbers can sometimes pose challenges, but having my older daughter participate helped balance things out. While the girls had their moments of struggle in navigating social situations, they eventually figured things out. It was heartening to see them interact, even though there were moments when one particular girl felt a bit left out or isolated from the main group.

It's worth reflecting on the fact that, for some of these girls, this might have been their first or second sleepover experience. By the time I was in 7th and 8th grade, I had already had numerous sleepovers, but these young teenagers had to put their social lives on hold for almost three years.

Part 3 - Changing the Future

In the summer of 2023, I embarked on a journey of self-improvement and self-care. It was a conscious decision. I felt ready to focus on myself and set goals. I began to feed my inner child, taking actions to enhance my physical and mental well-being. I spent quality time with myself, engaging in activities like kayaking, flint knapping, organizing, and writing. I took deep breaths and embraced the process of taking baby steps.

Once I felt that I had my own well-being on the right track, my attention turned to my family. It wasn't a deliberate process but rather a natural response to their needs. Seeing my family in pain, I felt a strong desire to help.

By the time my daughter had her birthday party, I had started writing this book. It enabled me to reflect on our situation and set goals for the future. My wife was ahead of me in terms of goal setting, and we began to discuss ways to improve our family's well-being.

My wife and I engaged in more conversations about getting our family back on track. We recognized that our daughters were dealing with chronic stress, and we were constantly striving to help them navigate it. Sometimes they were open to discussing and working on it, while other times it felt overwhelming.

I felt like I was finally taking care of myself and moving toward a future I was enthusiastic about. Naturally, I wanted to bring my family along with me. I observed my daughters spending most of their days on screens and ending the day frustrated, bored, and upset.

I initially attempted to include our daughters in my activities and asked if they wanted to participate. They usually declined, leaving me feeling frustrated. My wife pointed out that I was asking them to engage in "my" activities – things I wanted – rather than considering their desires. She was right, and I knew I needed to change my approach.

I started by limiting screen time and providing them with two choices, two alternatives to the screen. For example, "You can do the dishes or help me grocery shop." This was an improvement, but still not the best approach. We were thinking differently, speaking a different language, and it remained a work in progress. Eventually, we began to develop a shared language, and our family, our community, began to function more harmoniously.

One of our most significant successes was initiated by our youngest daughter. She played a key role in shaping our future. After dinner, when we asked what everyone wanted to do, our youngest suggested playing games. Even though I was tired and initially hesitant, my wife was eager to participate. We moved to the dining room table and discussed which game we should play. It was a discussion, with different preferences in mind. My youngest daughter's favorite game is Harry Potter Clue, while my oldest daughter's favorite is Monopoly. My wife and I collectively decided on Harry Potter Headbands. It turned out to be one of the most enjoyable nights of the summer. We played through the entire deck, spending hours laughing and giggling together.

It was a fantastic experience. I went from being a bit of a curmudgeon on the sofa to giggling like a child. My youngest daughter broke the ice and set us on a new path. It was a remarkable win. Recently, we've switched to playing cards. Euchre, my wife's family card game, is something I wanted our daughters to learn. I love it! Everyone is learning strategy and critical thinking, and we discuss our hands after each play. It models life lessons, goal setting, reflection, and it's incredibly fun.

Every family has to find their own way to break the ice. Maybe your family is passionate about music, and you could have family band time. Perhaps storytelling, picture shows, movies, or shows are your thing. The key is to make time for your family and make it enjoyable. Discover what your family values and bring that into your quality time. Personally, I feel much better after game night, and I eagerly anticipate the next one, even if I lose. The joy is in the playing.

Once we had everyone engaged in our family community, we shifted our focus to our daughters' other communities – their friends, sports, and the upcoming school year.

It would be wonderful if every family could sit down at their dinner tables and create lists of the good, the bad, and the future. You could fold your paper into three sections, label them as "the good," "the bad," and "the future," and then all write and share your thoughts. However, I know this might not be feasible for everyone.

Instead, you must determine what works for your family. What is your family missing, and what are your core values? If these are being addressed within your family, you can also apply them to your interactions with other communities. Keep in mind that our kids missed out on nearly three years of social experiences and milestones. Engaging with their communities should be deliberate, with clear goals in mind. We need to be our children's life coaches now more than ever.

For my oldest daughter, who is in high school, playing ice hockey, and having a stable friend group, we find it most helpful to talk to her about goals and expectations. We help her reflect on recent events, and we incorporate our core values into these conversations. I believe most parents do this, but it is especially important now, given how much was missed in the past years. I revisit our core principles as frequently as possible.

My youngest daughter is in eighth grade, her friend groups are in transition, and she's quieter. It's sometimes difficult to notice her struggles until she's in tears. The first time this happened was a wake-up call for us. Reflecting on the past three years, we should have seen it coming. We've been actively searching for communities for her to join, and she's started playing field hockey, which appears to be helping. We've also had numerous discussions about friendships, exploring what makes a good and bad friend. But the wounds are deep, and the hurts are real. She is seeing the impact of actions firsthand. She sees and feels the pain of her friends. She has her own pains. As she struggles to find herself and build her friend groups, we can help reinforce our values.

Kids are trying to figure everything out. They're working hard to gain peer attention and rebuild the communities they've lost. However, they're making many mistakes, as we all do. The issue is that everyone is confused, and their peers are reinforcing all sorts of behaviors, not just the appropriate ones.

We learned these things on the playground, during recess, at family picnics. Kids learned them on TikTok and social media. We locked our kids away for seventeen months and gave them a screen. We gave them the social media substitute. This substitute reminds me of the scene in *Harry Potter* when his wand selects him. Ollivander says, "I think we expect great things from you, Mr. Potter... After all, He-Who-Must-Not-Be-Named did great things—Terrible, yes, but great" (Rowling 85).

The screen, the social media substitute, did great things for our children, but it also did terrible things. Social media allows our children to see horrible behavior, but very rarely the consequences. They don't feel the pain of the action, they don't have any guilt or ownership, so they don't understand it is wrong.

Our children didn't have to face the consequences of their actions on social media. In fact, they often get likes. When children returned to in-person instruction, they acted like school was social media, they continued to behave how their social media substitute taught them to behave. What do I have to do to get likes? How do I go viral? After so long in isolation, they believed this was the best way to get the attention they so desperately desired. But school is a real community, and it has rules. The actions that get likes on social media usually destroy the community. The community is a "we" not an "I." The community cannot function when everyone needs to be the center of attention. The community cannot function when its members don't value and respect each other.

Our children need to be retaught how to behave in communities. They need to be taught that social media is not the whole story, just a small piece. They need to understand that there are rules and if they break them, they will be held accountable. They need to know their actions are associated with physical or emotional pain to their community members, and their community members will remember this tomorrow. Our children are having trouble processing this. They are confused; we have changed the rules too many times. For the first time in months, our children are being held accountable for their actions by their peers and teachers. Our peers and teachers are not social media, and the actions that get "likes" on social media usually break down our friend groups, our learning communities, our sports teams, and our clubs. It is time to retrain, reteach and coach our students.

Understanding what our children have been through is the first part of this process. The second part is understanding where our children are physically and mentally. The final part is the plan to move forward. We are the parents, we are the trainers, the teachers, and the coaches for our children. We got this! We have been doing it since our children were born, most of us even before that. Let's dive into the development of our child.

Chapter 9
Biology, Cognitive Development, Motivation, and Personality

It has been a long time since my class in college that focused on psychosocial development. Let's take the time to revisit and refresh our understanding of childhood development theories in light of the challenges children have faced over the past few years. This deeper understanding can provide valuable insights into how children may have been affected by the pandemic and what they might need moving forward.

Piaget's stages of Cognitive Development, Maslow's hierarchy of needs, and Erikson's stages of emotional development are foundational theories in the field of child psychology. They offer essential frameworks for understanding how children develop cognitively, emotionally, and socially.

For anyone interested in exploring these theories further or delving into child psychology, I have cited all the websites and books that I used. A simple google search started the ball rolling. The websites below are excellent starting points, and I also recommend the book "Educational Learning Theories" by Molly Zhou and David Brown. This book is part of the creative commons **CC BY-NC-SA**. It is a valuable resource for aspiring and current teachers or parents seeking to develop their understanding of these theories and their practical applications.

These are the websites that I relied on. If this section makes you hungry for more information, or if your children are younger or older than school age, I would encourage you to explore them:

- **Verywell Mind**
- **Psychcentral**
- **Maryville University**
- **SimplyPsychology**

Again, like I said in the introduction, I am an outdoor school teacher making observations and connections to support my students and daughters. I am not a doctor. I am just going to talk about the big ideas and highlight the connections I have made.

Revisiting these ideas with a purpose and thinking about how they apply to our students post pandemic has been exciting. I can see where they are stuck and what they need to work on to move forward faster. This is only a scratch on the surface of these ideas, but it is important. Understanding where our children were before the pandemic will help us understand what they missed. It has also given me patience and hope. I now know why my students are acting a certain way, and I can address their needs and move forward.

As a parent taking the time to read this book, your commitment to ongoing learning and your dedication to helping children navigate these challenging times are commendable. It's through a deeper exploration of child development that we can better support and nurture the well-being and growth of our children.

Structuring our support for our child's developmental needs will enhance our results. If our child is working on coordination, we should not be trying to work on strength. Instead, we should work on body awareness and balance. Likewise, if our child is working on autonomy, we should not force them to follow our steps to complete a task but rather allow them the freedom to discover their own way.

As human beings, we are inherently social and emotional creatures, wired to establish connections with others. We mimic facial expressions and sounds. We seek out conversations and peer groups. We long for physical contact from other humans.

These connections are so significant that isolation can be used as a form of punishment and even torture. Remember being little and being sent to your room, or time out. Amish shun members that don't want to be part of their community. Our prison system uses solitary confinement for prisoners that misbehave, and this form of punishment has been shown to have long-lasting harm on inmates. (Herring; "Solitary Confinement").

Social distancing was not the same as solitary confinement, but it seemed close. If you were lucky, you were part of a large family. If you were unlucky, you were living alone. We could still access people via phones and trips to the store, but we are social creatures, and the shutdown had an impact on us. During the pandemic, our children not only changed biologically, but their metal development was also impacted.

Part 1 – Biological Development

Our biological development unfolds in a predictable pattern, encompassing stages from conception to birth, through childhood and puberty, into young adulthood, and eventually into old age and the inevitable finality of death. Within this overarching trajectory, we encounter distinct phases, each marked by characteristic features as well as unique challenges and stresses. It is challenging to discuss the physical aspects of development without acknowledging the concurrent mental and social dimensions.

At the very beginning, we all commence as a fertilized egg. During my wife's pregnancy, I subscribed to a website that provided weekly updates on our baby's progress—how big our baby had become and what milestones were being achieved. Every Friday morning, these updates became our main topic of conversation. I remember one of my favorites was the comparison to a jicama, an unusual root vegetable. Not only did I learn what it looked like, but I also took the time to master its pronunciation. It was fascinating to contemplate the weekly transformations in our child's development—perhaps a heartbeat one week, the growth of tiny fingers the next, and the emergence of eyes another. Witnessing the rapid pace of change was both thrilling and awe-inspiring.

After our daughters were born, we regularly visited the doctors for developmental assessments. These assessments served as a kind of report card to gauge their progress. I recall my wife diligently reviewing the results, always striving to understand how we could support our daughters in achieving even better scores. Major milestones such as holding their heads up, rolling over, crawling, sitting, walking, and eventually talking all occurred within defined age ranges. It was comforting to know that growth follows a predictable trajectory.

Babies experience a period of unparalleled physical growth during their first four years of life. From a single fertilized egg, they evolve into complex multicellular beings capable of walking, talking, and interpreting the world around them. At around four years of age, this breakneck pace of physical growth begins to taper off, only to be reignited during puberty. Puberty marks the final intense phase of physical development, lasting anywhere from two to five years. During this stage, individuals undergo the development of secondary sexual characteristics. It's worth noting that even after puberty concludes, a young person's adult body is still in the process of maturation.

Young adulthood typically begins around eighteen or nineteen years of age, though some argue that this phase can extend into one's mid to late twenties. Notably, brain development continues until approximately age twenty-four. This stage can persist until around the age of forty, when individuals transition into middle adulthood. Middle adulthood continues until roughly the age of sixty-five, at which point we enter the phase of late adulthood. This natural progression through life stages underscores the intricate and remarkable journey of human growth and development (Zhou and Brown).

Growth is a concept that's straightforward to grasp— it's predictable, continuous, and universal. We all experience growth and eventually face the inevitability of aging and mortality. However, what isn't so constant and predictable is how we develop our sense of motivation, personality, and self-identity. This complex process has given rise to various theories, sparking debates about whether our inherent nature or our environment predominantly shapes us.

In our exploration of these intricate matters, we'll focus on three key theoretical frameworks: Piaget's theory of cognitive development, Maslow's hierarchy of needs, and Erikson's model of human development. These frameworks serve as valuable tools for constructing a holistic understanding of what our children might be grappling with and what they may have potentially lost during these challenging times.

Piaget's theory delves into the development of our cognitive faculties, emphasizing how our brains evolve.

Maslow's theory centers on motivation, while Erikson's theory revolves around personality development. What ties these theories together is the notion of stages, each building upon the previous one, and the idea that environmental influences shape our progression through these stages. However, each theory places its distinct emphasis on different facets of development: the ability to think, the drive for motivation, and the formation of personality.

It's important to note that these theories provide a valuable foundation for understanding the complexities of human development, but they do not represent an exhaustive list of factors. Nevertheless, delving into these ideas proved invaluable when attempting to comprehend the challenges our children are currently facing and the potential areas in which they may require support. These are ideas that I thought were important while I was trying to figure out why our kids are broken.

Part 2 – Cognitive development

Jean Piaget formulated the concept of four stages in mental growth. The first stage is the sensorimotor stage, which spans from birth to around two years of age. The second stage is the preoperational stage, covering roughly 18 months to seven years of age. The third stage is the concrete operational stage, lasting from seven years until about eleven years old. The final stage is the formal operational stage, which extends from eleven years of age throughout one's lifetime. These age ranges are average guidelines, with individual variations in developmental speed. Piaget asserted that brain development unfolds in a sequential manner, with each stage building upon the previous one, and skipping a stage is not possible. Furthermore, each stage brings new cognitive abilities.

During the sensorimotor stage, from birth to approximately 24 months, our cognitive development is focused on immediate sensory experiences. Initially, we can only comprehend what is directly in front of us—things we can see, touch, taste, and manipulate. At this point, the world is an extensive experiment, as we explore through trial and error. Young infants have not yet grasped the concept of object permanence, which is why games like peekaboo are so entertaining to them. They believe that when something is hidden, it disappears. However, around seven to nine months of age, object permanence begins to emerge. By the end of this stage, language development commences.

The preoperational stage, spanning from approximately 18 months to about seven years old, marks the period when we begin to understand that words and images can represent objects and concepts in the world around us. This stage witnesses the development of symbolic thinking skills, improved memory, and enhanced imagination. While children in this stage make progress in comprehending past and future events, the concept of time remains a considerable challenge for most. Thinking during this stage primarily relies on intuition, with initial thoughts often considered to be the correct ones. Cause and effect, time, and comparisons can still pose difficulties for children in this stage.

Between the ages of seven and eleven, individuals enter the concrete operational stage of brain development. During this phase, thinking shifts toward considering other people's perspectives and recognizing the uniqueness of one's feelings. Concrete logical thinking begins to emerge, marked by a literal interpretation of language—what is said is precisely what is meant. However, abstract or hypothetical thinking remains a challenge. Abstract reasoning, speculation, and predictions typically elude children in this stage.

The final stage of brain development is the formal operational stage, which typically commences around age eleven and extends throughout one's lifetime. During this phase, individuals begin to use symbols to understand abstract ideas and relationships. Systematic thinking and contemplation of abstract connections become possible. Complex subjects like algebra, chemistry, and poetry become more meaningful and comprehensible. While the formal operational stage is the last in Piaget's theory, he believed that brain development continues throughout life, largely influenced by the accumulation of knowledge (Zhou and Brown).

Piaget's work also delves into the concept of schemas, which serve as cognitive thought processes or building blocks essential for navigating complex situations. Schemas are "an up to date set of instructions and ideas about as much of the world as possible" (Smith). Schemas are dynamic and adapt as we encounter various life experiences, a process he referred to as assimilation. As we grow and encounter new experiences, our schemas must evolve and adapt to accommodate these novel situations ("Piaget").

Reflecting on my journey as a parent, I initially placed a strong emphasis on the early stages of my children's development, attending birthing classes and medical appointments with the hope of nurturing their intelligence and learning capabilities. However, as my daughters grew and life's demands took center stage, I shifted my focus towards celebrating their newfound discoveries and accomplishments.

Considering the pivotal role of formal education in shaping our cognitive abilities and leveraging the stages of brain development to facilitate learning, I can't help but empathize with students who may have missed out on essential early educational experiences. The thought of children bypassing critical phases, such as kindergarten and first grade, which mark the transition from the preoperational to the concrete operational stage of cognitive development, is alarming.

Think about all things we learned in kindergarten. I remember playing with blocks; I loved it. I wanted to build the highest tower. I tried again and again. These repetitive activities build grit and mental toughness. I was learning that I could have a positive impact on my environment. I learned to plan, take my time, and place the block precisely in the right spot. But most importantly, I was learning to learn from my mistakes. Some of our children missed 17 months of this, and it was replaced by digital learning.

Imagine being a kindergartener attempting to navigate this educational journey in the digital realm, where virtual teachers and online classes replace traditional classroom settings.

I have cherished memories of participating in hands-on activities, like counting bundles of straws. I remember witnessing the joy on my daughter's face as she engaged with her peers in learning. However, we now face the daunting task of supporting a generation of students who developed, or tried to develop, these crucial skills and cognitive schemas without the physical presence of a teacher or the camaraderie of classmates.

This realization underscores the urgency of finding innovative and effective strategies to support cognitive development in non-traditional learning environments. As parents, we play a crucial role in providing our children with opportunities for hands-on learning, critical thinking, and problem-solving, both within and outside the traditional classroom setting.

Part 3 – Motivation

Abraham Maslow's hierarchy of needs is often represented as a pyramid (Figure 9-1), with each level building upon the one below it. The foundational level, at the bottom of the pyramid, focuses on survival and includes physiological needs such as food, water, air, sleep, and clothing. According to Maslow's theory, individuals must fulfill these basic physiological needs before they can address the needs at higher levels. The second level, safety, pertains to security in terms of one's home, job, health, resources, and family. Once these safety needs are met, individuals can progress to the third level, love and belonging, which involves forming personal connections with family, friends, significant others, and communities. Beyond that, the fourth level is esteem, encompassing self-respect, strength, and freedom. At the apex of the pyramid is the fifth level, self-actualization, where individuals realize their full potential (Zhou and Brown, "Maslow's").

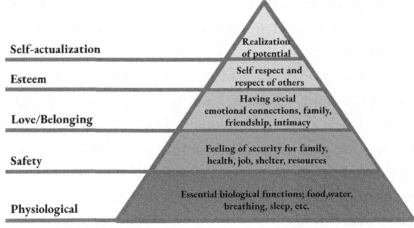

Figure 9-1. Maslow's Hierarchy of Needs

Personally, I find the concept of these hierarchical needs to be fundamental to education. Schools often provide free or reduced meals because it's challenging for students to learn if their basic physiological needs, like hunger, are not met. Furthermore, structured classrooms with clear procedures create a safe environment for building communities. Structure gives the student an understanding of how the classroom works and how they can contribute. A constant structure develops trust and stability. This feeling develops confidence, and students feel safe interacting with teachers and peers. Positive support encourages students to be the best version of themselves. They know they are valued and that their voice is important and unique.

In my 27 years of working with students, I've observed a pattern: the top 10% of students tend to have their basic needs on the lower levels of the pyramid already met. Consequently, they can focus on building communities, establishing relationships, striving for respect, and developing their potential without the distraction of unmet physiological or safety needs.

On the other hand, the bottom 10% of students often find themselves stuck at the lower levels of the pyramid. If they struggle to access food and water, it's difficult to motivate them to think about anything else. Some of these students rely on school for their only meals. Additionally, those who have met their basic biological needs may still feel unsafe due to circumstances like homelessness, parental abuse, or bullying in their neighbourhood. In some cases, students may act out at school because it's the one place where they have some semblance of control in their lives.

It's important to note that these are generalizations, and individuals are complex with unique circumstances. While there may be variations and criticisms of Maslow's hierarchy, the underlying idea of addressing basic needs as a foundation for motivation remains an essential consideration in education and human development.

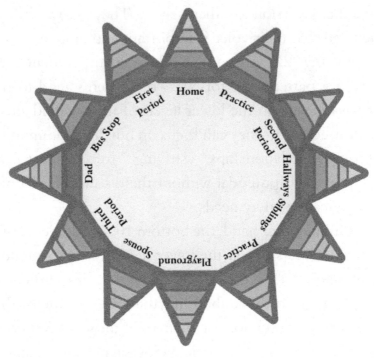

Figure 9-2 Maslow's Star

I'm not an expert in Maslow's theory but, I have accumulated over 27 years of experience in motivating students and athletes. In my view, if we were to closely examine a group of people, we might discover a model that resembles a circle covered with pyramids rather than a strict hierarchical pyramid. More like Maslow' Star (Figure 9-2). It's conceivable that each environment or significant person in our lives could be represented by its own pyramid. In reality, our position on these pyramids may shift as we transition from one environment to another. We may have our basic needs met in one place but not in another, feel safe in one but not in another, or have a strong sense of community in one while lacking it in another.

The most successful individuals are those who understand which environment can fulfill which of Maslow's needs. They are adept at shifting their focus and embracing the needs that each environment offers. For example, someone might feel safe in a science class, enabling them to make friends and gain respect, while feeling unsafe in a language arts class, prompting them to lay low and concentrate on coping strategies.

During the pandemic, I did not feel secure in my job, and that sense of insecurity impacted various aspects of my life. Fear permeated different environments, and I carried it with me everywhere. Human beings are complex, we are constantly processing information and adjusting our needs and motivations.

By initially focusing on the simplified single-pyramid model, we can gain valuable insights into the motivations and needs of our children and ourselves. Once this insight is gained, a closer examination is often necessary for a more complete picture. For instance, we might wonder why someone excels in science class but struggles in language arts. In some cases, it may be due to an underlying fear or anxiety related to a specific environment.

In the example of my oldest daughter starting high school in the 2022-2023 school year, she initially felt terrified and unsafe because she didn't know anyone. She was operating on the second level of the pyramid. It took about a month for her to find a sense of safety at school, with the biggest issue being lunchtime when she had no one to eat with. After reaching out to friends and friends of friends, we managed to find her a group to eat with after the first couple of days. However, she didn't truly feel safe for at least a month, and perhaps even longer. This fear and anxiety significantly shaped her daily experiences, and as parents, it was heart-wrenching for my wife and me. We were aware of the problem and did our best to help address it, but not all fears are as readily identifiable and solvable.

Thinking back to March 2020, the pandemic prompted us to shut down everything that wasn't deemed essential. We instructed everyone to practice social distancing and later to wear masks. This created a pervasive sense of unease and danger, leading us to dismantle the communities we belonged to, except for our immediate families. Our playgrounds and peer interactions were essentially eliminated.

We implemented dashboards to track the number of COVID-19 cases and fatalities; it was difficult to feel safe. I vividly recall stories of New York creating portable morgues, with even an ice rink near my location being converted into a morgue. It was a truly frightening time. Jobs were shuttered, parks were closed, and communities felt as though they were cancelled. We were collectively trapped on the second level of Maslow's hierarchy of needs as this pervasive fear eroded our sense of safety.

As restrictions eased and vaccines became available, some of the fear subsided, but new concerns emerged. Over the past three years, we've grappled not only with our own health but also the health of our loved ones. Questions arose about visiting grandparents, knowing who had contracted COVID-19, and grieving for those we had lost. We were all faced with decisions about what to do if we or our family members fell ill, whether schools would ever return to normal, and the stability of our jobs.

In addition to the ongoing public health crisis, we were bombarded with polarizing news stories and natural disasters. The news and social media played a role in exacerbating our feelings of insecurity. Messages about masks, police brutality, presidential elections, and the attack on the Capitol building added to our sense of unease. Droughts, wildfires, and extreme weather events seemed to punctuate the gaps between these social and political issues. Fear was ever-present, and it felt like it was being fed to us at every opportunity.

Thankfully, some individuals and programs sought to counter this by focusing on positive news and entertainment, providing a respite from the constant fear. My family found solace in watching *Some Good News* with John Krasinski. We also revisited *The Office* and indulged in binge-watching *Survivor*. These shows provided a much-needed escape from the overwhelming fear that surrounded us.

Every major transition during this period was marked by fear, whether it was social distancing, masks in public, or shifts in learning modalities (such as continuity of learning, distance learning, hybrid learning, or in-person learning with masks). The uncertainty left us wondering whether each new phase would be better or worse. It became challenging to embrace the third stage of Maslow's hierarchy, love and belonging, when the fear of being part of a group was so prevalent. Fear became a dominant motivator for nearly three years, and that is a difficult place to dwell for such an extended period.

Our children had to navigate and process all of these challenges. Some received filtered information from parents or guardians who processed the news and chose what to share with their children. Others had unrestricted access to news and social media, leaving them to make sense of the information on their own. While some issues, like natural disasters, were relatively straightforward, others, like political and social issues, were considerably more complex.

A good idea should undergo thorough discussion, be broken down, and have its details examined. The consequences should be discussed, and the idea should evolve through stakeholder input. If possible, it should be implemented. This is how we approach personal decisions, and it should also be the approach for ideas at all levels. Unfortunately, politics has eroded this process. The word "compromise" is missing. Respect between opposing sides has waned, and the focus has shifted from what's best for the country to simply winning at all costs. Fear has become their primary tool; sown in every corner they touch.

It's no wonder that our children, and even I, grapple with anxiety. Fear is incessantly fed to us by the news, social media, and our leaders. To make matters worse, our leaders started labelling everything as "fake news," leaving us unsure of what to believe or whom to trust. The foundation of safety on Maslow's second level has crumbled.

Personally, I've chosen to disengage from this cycle of fear. I limit my news consumption to written sources and only delve deeper if a topic genuinely piques my curiosity. I refrain from discussing ideas with people unless asked, but I enjoy engaging in conversations about ideas with people I respect. And, of course, I vote.

As a parent, I've been concerned with safety. Despite being a well-educated, successful adult with a loving family and multiple communities, I find myself struggling to digest and process facts from editorial opinions designed to incite fear. This is a powerful tool that the media and those in power use to manipulate us. My children are experiencing the same struggle. I witness their fear and anxiety in the quiet moments at the end of the day and the chaotic moments before school. If I look closely enough, I can almost always notice it.

Living in constant fear and seeking safety impacts our relationships, self-image, and our ability to reach our full potential. As parents, we navigate this challenge, and our children face it as learners, athletes, club members, and young adults. It is time to talk about our fears and anxieties in a positive, rational way. It is time to support our children as they start to address these issues so we can develop stronger communities and relationships. This will allow our children to regain their self-esteem and start working on being the best version of themselves.

Part 4 - Personality

Erik Erikson's model of human development offers one perspective on how individuals develop their personalities. While it's not the only way to understand this process, it serves as a valuable starting point.

Erikson formulated a theory that focuses on the major psychosocial conflicts people encounter throughout their lives and explores how these conflicts shape their personalities. Each conflict represents a person's needs conflicting with society's needs, and how individuals navigate and resolve these conflicts is reflected in their personality.

Erikson's theory comprises eight significant stages or conflicts, each of which serves as a fundamental building block in an individual's personality development. These stages overlap, and a person may work on several conflicts simultaneously. The notion is that successfully completing a stage leads to the development of a virtue or a higher moral standard, while failure to do so can compromise their ability to navigate subsequent stages (Cherry; "Erik"; Zhou and Brown). The stages are as follows:

1. **Trust vs. Mistrust** - Infancy (birth to 18 months)
2. **Autonomy vs. Shame and Doubt** - Toddlerhood (18 months to 3 years)
3. **Initiative vs. Guilt** - Preschool (3-5 years)
4. **Industry vs. Inferiority** - Early School Years (6-11 years)

5. **Identity vs. Role Confusion** - Adolescence (12-18 years)

6. **Intimacy vs. Isolation** - Young Adulthood (19-40 years)

7. **Generativity vs. Stagnation** - Middle Adulthood (40-65 years)

8. **Integrity vs. Despair** - Late Adulthood (65 to death)

It's important to note that these stages exist on a continuum; individuals are never wholly trusting or mistrusting, autonomous or filled with shame, etc. When a person successfully completes a stage, they experience a sense of accomplishment, often referred to as an ego strength or virtue. Conversely, an individual who does not navigate a stage successfully may experience a lack of confidence in that particular area. Erikson's research provides a solid foundation for understanding how self-esteem develops in relation to one's relationship with society and the formation of their personality.

In the context of school-age children, I'd like to explore conflicts 3, 4, and 5, as these stages are particularly relevant during this period of development.

Stage Three: Initiative vs Guilt

Stage three unfolds in children aged three to five years old. During this phase, children are wrestling with the question of whether it's acceptable to act, to explore, and to assert themselves ("Human Development"; "Erik"). It's also a stage where parents can start assigning responsibilities and encourage children to participate in planning and decision-making, such as helping with chores, selecting books, getting dressed, and establishing daily routines. At this age, children are actively trying to make sense of the world around them, often resorting to the ubiquitous "Why?" question.

Encouraging independence in children during this stage fosters the development of purpose and confidence. If parents are overly restrictive, dictating every action or criticizing their child's efforts, it may lead to feelings of guilt regarding their actions. Paradoxically, attempting to control children to ensure their success can have the opposite effect, undermining their independence and self-assuredness. While some level of parental guidance and reflection is important, overly controlling or harshly critical feedback is counterproductive.

Preschool and kindergarten are the foundational stages where children are primed to succeed in school, sports, and life. This phase requires social interaction with caregivers and peers, allowing children the freedom to make mistakes and understand cause-and-effect relationships. It's also essential for them to experience the consequences of overstepping boundaries. Engaging in household tasks and assisting others builds confidence and self-esteem. The handling of failure by peers and caregivers can either serve as a tool for developing mental resilience or as a weapon that damages one's self-image.

Consider playground scenarios as an example. We've all encountered a child who constantly changes the rules of a game to secure victory, ultimately leading to others quitting and the rule maker asking, "Why does everyone stop playing when I modify the rules?" This loss of playmates due to the child's unwillingness to cooperate can lead to feelings of guilt.

However, it's essential to note that this guilt differs from being found "guilty" in a criminal sense. Instead, it signifies acknowledging that you did something wrong, got caught, and are responsible for potentially harming friends or yourself. Parents can assist their children in processing this guilt, encouraging reflection on the outcomes and exploring alternative approaches for the future.

With proper support, this guilt becomes a driving force for building a confident child who understands when to assert leadership and when to listen to peers. This confidence facilitates problem-solving and persistence, even in the face of setbacks, contributing to the development of mental toughness. These children recognize that failure can yield valuable lessons and the opportunity for improvement. They develop the skills to succeed within the confines of a fair game, fostering grit and tenacity.

Simple tasks, such as pouring their own drink, can either instill a profound sense of accomplishment or, if they spill it, result in a crushing sense of defeat. Success signifies responsibility for meeting their own needs and independence. Failure, however, can induce guilt. How this guilt is handled by caregivers and peers plays a critical role. Supportive responses, such as, "Everyone spills drinks sometimes. What could you do differently next time?" motivate children to persevere and improve.

Conversely, if guilt is imposed by overbearing caregivers or manipulative peers, it can lead to the development of a guarded, introverted personality. Such negative interactions can shatter a child's confidence and deter them from asserting their ideas and thoughts, fostering a fear of attempting new challenges. This emotional bullying may drive the child into a shell, undermining their motivation to try, and potentially leading to feelings of shame, a belief that their very being is flawed.

Building strong peer and caregiver relationships that emphasize kindness in the face of mistakes is essential for nurturing initiative. These communities working together help teach positive self-reflection and self-talk. These communities are essential in helping develop this virtue. A simple phrase or sincere encouragement at the right moment can significantly contribute to building this trait in our children. Some children missed this for almost seventeen months. We need to reengage our children into positive communities so they can be exposed to this support system as soon as possible.

Stage Four: Industry vs. Inferiority

Stage four encompasses children aged five to twelve years old. During this stage, your child is navigating the question of whether they can find success in the world of people and events (Sus). Social interaction plays a crucial role in this stage. Children begin to compare themselves to their peers, assessing who's the tallest, fastest, or smartest. These comparisons help them gauge their position within the peer group ("Human Development"; "Erik").

Positive reinforcement from parents, teachers, and peers plays a pivotal role in developing a positive sense of industry during this stage. Industry refers to the ability to feel confident in one's skills and tasks, set meaningful goals, and believe in their abilities. It involves growing their confidence, successfully completing tasks, and striving toward objectives. Conversely, if a child receives little to no positive feedback and is consistently exposed to negative feedback, they may develop feelings of inferiority and a lack of self-confidence.

This phase is about learning and fostering confidence, not arrogance. It's about developing a desire to excel while understanding that hard work can lead to improvement. Failure is an essential part of this process, but the support provided is even more critical. When a child faces failure, it should be seen as an opportunity for growth and self-improvement, not as a discouragement of their efforts. Children naturally aim to please their teachers, peers, and parents, and if they consistently fall short of expectations, they may develop a sense of inferiority.

Inferiority can arise when a child is discouraged from using or developing their skills. Negative statements like "You're not good at this," "You should quit," or "Your efforts are never enough" can be damaging. This relates to the concept of mindsets: if a child is surrounded by individuals with a growth mindset, they understand that practice can lead to improvement and that they can develop skills over time. In contrast, if they are surrounded by those with a deficient mindset who make excuses for their lack of skills, the child might never acquire those skills. This can hinder their problem-solving abilities and prevent the development of self-confidence and self-esteem. If a child consistently falls short of expectations, they may struggle with self-confidence, academics, and social interactions in the long term.

There are three keys to building industrial children:

1. **Your Brain is Like a Muscle**: The brain, like a muscle, becomes stronger with use. Encouraging children to think independently, make connections, and ask for help can make learning a fun and exciting process.

2. **Embrace Your Superpower**: Children have unique qualities, charisma, and leadership abilities. When used correctly, these attributes can be powerful. It's crucial to celebrate and acknowledge them. When your child misuses their superpower, guidance and redirection are necessary.

3. **Small Attainable Goals**: Setting small, achievable goals can help children build confidence, mental toughness, and a sense of industry. Encourage them to celebrate their accomplishments, no matter how small they may seem.

Children are truly remarkable, and each one has their own unique spark or superpower. It's crucial for adults to recognize and celebrate these qualities when they are used correctly. However, it's equally important to guide and redirect children when they use these attributes inappropriately.

When children use their superpowers positively, it's an opportunity to reinforce their self-esteem and sense of belonging. Recognizing their achievements and unique qualities helps them feel valued and accepted in their peer groups. By celebrating their excellence, we send a message that they have what it takes to thrive in this world, which boosts their confidence.

As an educator, parent, or caregiver, when you witness a child excelling or demonstrating a unique talent, call it a superpower. Help them understand that not everyone possesses the same abilities, and what comes naturally to them may be challenging for others. In fact, what seems to come natural to some people might actually be the result of hard work. This superpower might be the result of years of practice. Acknowledging this skill and celebrating it empowers our children. Encouraging them to embrace their strengths and channel them positively shows then they are a valued part of our community. Their skill can help make our community stronger. Ultimately, acknowledging and celebrating their superpowers can foster a strong sense of self and contribute to their personal growth and development.

Stage Five: Identity vs Role Confusion

Stage five of Erikson's psychosocial development theory occurs during adolescence, typically spanning from ages twelve to eighteen. This stage revolves around self-exploration as individuals cope with questions about their identity and values. Adolescents strive to understand who they are and what holds significance for them, a process that can be both exhilarating and challenging ("Human Development"; "Erik").

During this stage, young individuals embark on a quest to identify their personal values, set meaningful life goals, and explore their interests. It's akin to the Goldilocks dilemma, where too much freedom can overwhelm them, while too little can be stifling, potentially leading to role confusion. Adolescents need a balance between independence and the security of their family's support to navigate this stage successfully.

Peer groups gain prominence during this stage, often overshadowing parental influence in the eyes of adolescents. They experiment within their peer circles, trying various styles, values, and attitudes. Erikson is well-known for coining the term "identity crisis" to describe the challenges faced during this stage.

This phase involves numerous changes, both physical and emotional, as adolescents navigate the complexities of puberty. They contend with the transformation into adulthood while still discovering their true selves. Important decisions about their future, such as college or trade school, career aspirations, and religious beliefs, are on the horizon, and they are actively trying to make sense of it all.

The confusion that comes during this stage occurs in multiple settings all at once. Confusion about talents, friends, parents, and the future blooms. This confusion is multiplied exponentially when our child discovers they don't fit into classical categories.

As parents we must give them the freedom to work out this confusion. Independence is a critical aspect of this stage, but it should be accompanied by the safety net of family support. We have to give them love and understanding so they know they can still come to us and talk about it. This gives them the freedom to experiment and make choices. It allows them to build healthy strategies to deal with their confusion instead of self-destructive ones.

In the context of this stage, the term "fidelity" is often used, representing the idea of being true to oneself in a world filled with contradictions. It's worth noting that this stage doesn't come to an abrupt end at age eighteen; it continues to evolve, influenced by an individual's support network, curiosity, and intelligence. Smarter individuals may take longer to fully grasp their identity.

Erikson's stages of development build upon each other, and this stage draws upon the skills and experiences accumulated during earlier stages (Cherry; "Erik"; Zhou and Brown). While it can be terrifying, it's also an exciting journey of self-discovery.

Reflecting on my high school years, I went through a transformative process. As a freshman and sophomore, I disliked school, but in my junior year, I was starting to find my way. By my senior year, I had turned things around and embraced the opportunities school had to offer. College was where I truly figured out who I was and what I wanted to pursue, with the support of great teachers and friends, some of whom may not have even realized their influence.

I can't fathom the impact of losing the high school experience to the COVID-19 pandemic, but as parents, we can strive to help our children find equivalent experiences and support their growth. It's crucial to understand what was lost and the importance of those experiences, and then actively seek out and encourage new opportunities to replace them.

Part 5 - Reflection

What does all of this mean, and why is it important? In simple terms, our children have continued to grow and develop during the pandemic. Their environments were altered, their peers and caregivers (including teachers, grandparents, and coaches) were removed, and they had to adapt to new circumstances or make do with what they had. While they may appear older, many are still navigating how to process their new surroundings, interact with their peers, and understand themselves. They require structured support, compassionate hearts, and understanding caregivers, peers, and teachers.

Now is the time to hit the reset button and work with a sense of purpose to help our children address the needs that may have been unmet. If we don't step in, they will find ways to cope on their own. Unfortunately, sometimes our children's coping mechanisms are unhealthy or destructive ("Teens"). However, as mentors and caregivers, our involvement can expedite the development of the healthy skills they need to navigate our communities and pursue their dreams.

On a deeper level, it's essential to recognize that our children not only missed out on peer interaction and teacher praise but also turned to social media to fill those gaps. Likes on social media platforms often became a substitute for peer approval, and they may not have been aware that social media represents only a small fraction of individuals seeking attention.

I recall being taught as a child that television is a realm of make-believe and that attempting to emulate actions seen on TV could lead to harm. We learned that humans cannot fly, and death is final. Social media, on the other hand, has evolved into a platform for bullying, trolling, and hate. How does one achieve likes on social media? By being outrageous, provocative, or risky. Social media has, in some ways, replaced our peers, and it can be ruthless and indifferent to our feelings.

The consequences of this shift to screens remain largely hidden from view. As parents we need to address this. We need to reduce the influence the social media substitute has on our kids. Small steps, small goals. We can have device-free dinner, or other forced family fun with no phones. We can have conversations about things that our kids see on social media. We can limit apps and screen time. We can remove apps altogether. We can have a "no phone until chores are done" rule. It is hard to be consistent, but as parents we must.

As communities strive to rebuild, they often struggle to regain a sense of normalcy, which can impact how they function. I've witnessed this in both school and in the ice hockey locker room, and I've been part of it. The desire for things to return to normal can sometimes overshadow the effort needed for success. I've quickly remembered how to adapt to my communities because of my age and experience, but our children are still young. They may not have had the opportunity to thoroughly learn these lessons about how to act in different situations, or they might have learned them but forgotten them. By not reteaching etiquette, we have set our children up for failure.

We have a substantial amount of work ahead of us, but we've been doing it since our children were born. For those who may not have been as actively involved before, now is the chance to hit the reset button and make a positive impact.

Chapter 10
Retrain, Reteach, and Coach

It is true that our children are facing challenges. They missed out on crucial peer interactions during their developmental stages, impacting their autonomy, initiative, industry, and identity formation. Many might find themselves stuck at stages two or three of Maslow's hierarchy of needs. Safety can be elusive, and even if they do feel safe now, they must reintegrate into the communities they've lost. They are searching for their playgrounds while possibly struggling with cognitive development. They have lost skills, confidence, and grit.

We all need to adopt a growth mindset, believing that we can make things better. With this mindset, we can address negative interactions and fears that have accumulated over the last three years. Yes, our children face difficulties, but they are resilient and remarkable. They remain full of excitement and optimism, still driven by curiosity, and we, as parents, are here to support them.

Recognizing that everyone is feeling some level of confusion and disconnection empowers us to move forward. That's what we are all striving for at this moment—rebuilding our communities and rediscovering our playgrounds. From small groups to larger ones, our children are dealing with defining boundaries, determining what's appropriate and what's not.

As parents, it is our responsibility to be there for our children, guiding them to become successful contributors to their communities. We are their protectors, their primary life coaches, and their safe haven.

Our kids need our support now more than ever. It's time to hit the reset button and put our focus back on them. In times like these, I'm reminded of the wisdom of Lao Tzu: "A journey of a thousand miles begins with a single step." It's time for us to roll up our sleeves and plan how to help our children navigate the post-pandemic world. But how? Here's my best advice: We need to retrain, reteach, and coach our children.

Teaching has been a passion of mine since college. I discovered it during my chemistry classes when friends sought my help, and I knew how to assist them. I was fortunate to have exceptional science teachers in high school, and I developed a deep love for the subject. It made sense to me, and I could effectively explain complex concepts to my peers, connecting the dots.

My journey continued when I started working at summer camps. I was entrusted with a group of fourteen-year-olds, and I was responsible for creating and delivering lessons. I found immense joy in teaching. As the world faced a shortage of teachers, I realized how much I loved this vocation, and there was no turning back.

I not only love teaching but also admire the work of great educators. Observing how they hone their craft has been a source of inspiration for me. For over three decades, I've been a dedicated learner, passionate about understanding the art of learning.

One of the most impactful programs I've been a part of is first aid and CPR training. It equips you with essential skills to respond effectively in emergency situations. These skills are invaluable when facing crises and can help save lives. I've been participating in this training for over thirty years, and it continues to amaze me. They have a great method for teaching skills. They teach a skill, have you practice it, then teach another skill. As your skills build, they link them together to form skill sets.

These skills sets are then connected to teach caregivers how to respond to a person in need. The basic class can be completed in a long weekend, and you feel confident you know how to act in an emergency. For most of us, this is all we'll ever need, but if you take more classes, they start to coach you. How will you react in more and more environments with more and more emergencies? This is a perfect model for us as parents. What skills will our children use every day or every week? These are the skills we should focus on and group into skill sets. Once the skill sets are learned, then explore how they are connected and when they are used.

When my family adopted a dog during the pandemic, all of us took on the responsibility of learning how to train her. We turned to resources like Zac George's training methods on YouTube and the book *The Art of Raising a Puppy* by the Monks of New Skete. These resources emphasized the importance of creating a sense of community for our puppy, teaching us the "hows" and "whys" of dog training. One crucial lesson was establishing our dog as the lowest-ranking member of our family pack to prevent aggression toward younger family members. This insight was eye-opening, and it helped us foster a positive relationship with our dog.

While our children are not puppies, they are the youngest members of our family. They need to understand where they are in the family hierarchy. This structure needs to translate to all their communities. We need to train them how to act in all of their environments. When we go into public, this training needs to be reinforced, and this training needs to be revisited when skills diminish.

I also have experience as a coach, having worked with teams in various sports such as football, wrestling, lacrosse, and ice hockey. The American Development Model used by USA Hockey for coaching has been influential in my coaching journey. It emphasizes the qualities of a great coach and seeks to shift the focus from winning at all costs to making sports enjoyable again. This "great reset" aims to address why smaller countries produce more national hockey players than the United States. The answer lies in prioritizing fun and creativity in sports, rather than just focusing on winning.

I once heard a story about a highly successful wrestling program which produced numerous state championships, yet it lacked fans at matches. When a coach questioned an alumnus about his absence, the response was shocking: "I hate wrestling." All young kids love to wrestle, but this individual had been taught to hate it. This anecdote underscores how the coach drained the fun out of the sport, leading to a breakdown in the athletes' passion. It serves as a reminder that learning should be enjoyable. While it can be challenging at times, it should ultimately be exciting and engaging.

To navigate post-pandemic life and make a positive change, I propose a fundamental idea by Brian Stuart Germin: "Our body cannot go where the mind has not gone first."

I like this idea, but I rephrase it, "The body cannot go where the mind has not been." This idea revolves around preparing for the worst while hoping for the best, akin to first aid and CPR training. Knowing what to do in advance is crucial when facing an emergency. It requires the courage to take the first step when everything around you is in chaos. It is also why retraining in new environments is so important; it teaches us that this is how we act, regardless of where we are. I use guided visualization while preparing for new activities and important games. It helps focus my intent and prepare for high stress situations.

Right now, our kids are confused; they don't know our expectations. Our kids don't know how to act in their new communities, in these new environments, and they don't know how to treat real people; they have lost their grit. As parents we can help them. It is time for us to focus on three fundamental steps:

1. **Retrain**
2. **Reteach**
3. **Coach**

We need to retrain, reteach, and coach our kids. Simple, right? No! It is not simple, but we are parents, and we have been doing this from the beginning. We have experience. So, to give you a starting point for this seemingly daunting task, let's break down each of these skills.

Part 1 - Retraining

Training is the fundamental process of acquiring skills or knowledge. It involves the development of a particular skill or a set of related skills, a skill set. Whether it's first aid, CPR, lifeguarding, dog training, or teacher training, all of these involve mastering skills that can be applied repeatedly. This concept closely aligns with Piaget's Schema theory, where individuals learn to apply specific skills or skill sets based on the situations they encounter.

Our journey of training begins with our children from the moment we welcome them into the world. We teach them essential things like their names, our names, how to eat, how to dress, how to communicate, and how to read. We nurture them, giving them tummy time, reading them stories, and naming everything they touch. This process of training starts from the day they are born and continues for as long as they are with us.

As parents, we are intimately familiar with our children, and we have specific goals in mind for their development. It's time for us to press the reset button and rethink our approach to their training. We should begin with some fundamental values, such as reminding them to turn off their phones in a movie theater and refrain from throwing things at concerts. I would even urge them to turn off their phones at dinner. Then, we can delve into the complexities of what affects our children in today's world, understanding their need for peer validation and the freedom to explore. We can establish boundaries, much like invisible fences, specifying where and when certain behaviors are appropriate. Games with rules, clear expectations, and consequences all play a vital role in this process.

One common mistake is assuming that our children already possess certain skills, leading us to rush into teaching content without first ensuring they have a strong foundation of basic skills. In my first years of teaching, I made this mistake. I knew they learned graphing in middle school, so why should I spend time reteaching it? But they only knew how to graph, not when to use which type of graph. I battled this for a couple classes and then challenged them. By challenging them to prove what they knew about graphing, they became invested in the idea. The class was able to figure out which skills and connections were missing, and I could retrain them and teach them when to use which graph. The time spent retraining and teaching was a great investment and saved my students from frustration and poor performances on assignments.

Assuming skill mastery results in frustration for both parents and children. Let's prioritize teaching these fundamental life skills that are important to us as parents. If you believe your child already knows them, consider quizzing them to gauge their understanding. Ask them about your family's rules in various situations. If you are going to grandmas for lunch, ask them, "What do you say to grandma first? What do you say after dinner? What can you talk to grandma about? If you see grandma cleaning up, what should you do?" If they don't know, it's time to retrain. If they do know, consider making connections to other communities, revisiting, and reinforcing major skills and lessons.

Think about how many times you've reminded your child to look both ways before crossing the street, say "please" and "thank you," or clean up after themselves. These are skills we understand and practice. This is our wheelhouse as parents and caregivers. Now, retraining provides us with the opportunity to reinforce these concepts. Retraining is about honing and improving our skills.

When you train a dog, you start in a distraction-free environment, and then you gradually introduce new settings to reinforce the skill. Every time you change your environment, you need to retrain the skill. New pet owners are shocked that the dog will listen at home but not at the park. I have experienced this many times with our dog. The solution is simple retraining. Now when my dog gets out of the car I make her sit, stay, and come. This simple exercise is retraining; her skills have been reinforced, and she follows commands better.

This principle applies to human training as well. When you retrain for first aid and CPR, they revisit the skills and update any changes. This is the same with teacher training, and it should be the same for your family. Over time, as we grow and evolve as a family, we learn together and find ways to refine our skills, and perhaps develop new techniques. Let's take a cue from USA Hockey's American Development Model: training should be enjoyable whenever possible.

Training requires energy, focus, motivation, insight, and planning. It begins with identifying the needs and pinpointing the skills that are lacking. Just as Mary Poppins knew that "a spoonful of sugar helps the medicine go down," finding enjoyable ways to incorporate training into daily life can make the process smoother (*Mary Poppins* 32:20-32:26). For example, you can challenge your family to finish cleaning up before a song ends, turning it into a fun race.

For younger children, games work like magic. Games like "Simon says" emphasize listening and following directions, while "hide and seek" teaches them to be still and quiet. The "telephone game" reinforces listening and relaying information. The key is that these games should be played for fun, with an emphasis on sportsmanship, whether they win or lose.

With older children, focus on enhancing their social skills. Teach them how to interact respectfully with peers, even when they disagree, and how to conduct themselves in larger groups. Engage in conversations with your children, ask questions, and offer praise when deserved. This can boost their self-esteem and help them develop qualities like autonomy, industry, initiative, and identity.

Most of my retraining moments occur in the car or at bedtime, where distractions are minimized, and focus is heightened. My daughters, aged 15 and 13, are currently undergoing retraining in areas such as building and maintaining meaningful friendships. I've observed that odd-numbered groups of kids tend to lead to conflicts. Groups of three and five almost always end in a fight unless the group is solid. Each member has to be valued or the group will break down. It's essential to teach them how to manage small group dynamics effectively. This skill set needs to be retrained.

Additionally, I'm preparing them for situations when they are out in public with friends. As a parent, I often anticipate worst-case scenarios, such as my kids getting lost while their phone is dead, and I provide guidance on what to do if those situations occur. I encourage them to text me when they leave and arrive at locations, ensure they have money and know how to manage it, and ask them to communicate if they will be late. These are essential skills that many children lack, and it's crucial to equip them with these abilities.

One issue that has become prevalent among children is excessive screaming. High-pitched, bone-chilling screams have become alarmingly common. Recently, at our local fair, I saw two girls greet each other via screams, which scared a group of nearby cops. The cops were extremely upset, and I don't blame them. It's essential to teach our children that screaming should be a last resort, a signal of distress, rather than a casual form of communication. Screaming incites chaos. The story of the boy who cried wolf illustrates the importance of reserving screaming for genuine emergencies.

Furthermore, I am instilling the value of kindness in my daughters and students. Being kind is a skill that seems to have faded in today's world, where negative behaviors from "Karens" and "trolls" dominate social media, and even political leaders engage in name-calling and demeaning rhetoric. We must emphasize the "Golden Rule": treat others as you want to be treated. This principle must be retrained and reestablished in our society.

Retraining our children to navigate the world with empathy and respect will undoubtedly be a long and ongoing process. However, by taking small steps today, we can lay the foundation for a brighter and more compassionate future. It's time to embark on the journey of retraining our children.

Part 2 - Reteaching

Teaching involves not only imparting skills but also fostering an understanding of how these skills connect and can be combined to achieve goals. It delves into the "why" behind what we do, exploring the importance and effectiveness of certain approaches. Teaching is an ongoing process, a journey of continuous learning and improvement. Just as Piaget talked about assimilation, the application of schemas to new situations, teaching helps individuals assimilate knowledge faster and more effectively.

In the context of our children, it's crucial to reteach them our core values and the characteristics we hold dear. We should instill these values in them now, rather than waiting for some distant future. Teaching serves as an anchor, allowing these values to become an integral part of their thoughts and feelings. It transforms rote memorization into true understanding, enabling them to apply these values when the need arises, thus promoting success.

Throughout our lives, we encounter numerous teachers in various forms—parents, friends, and even adversaries—all contributing to our growth. My parents had moments of greatness that I still think about. Not so much direct instruction, but indirect instruction. Modeling values and virtues. The constant desire to be better today than yesterday, to take care of our needs, to explore, to learn.

Teaching is a pervasive force in our lives if we pause to observe and absorb the lessons. However, it can be challenging amidst the hustle and bustle of daily life. Yet the potential for teaching is always there, waiting for us to slow down and embrace it.

We all have the potential to become excellent teachers, and you might have already played this role numerous times in your life. Reflect on those instances when you didn't just convey a skill but also taught when and how to apply it. Consider a simple example, like instructing someone on using cutlery—forks, spoons, and knives—explaining how to hold them and their respective functions. Now, imagine giving your child three diverse items to eat: a sizable piece of cucumber, roasted potatoes, and cereal with milk. Challenge your child to consume these foods with their new tools. This is where your teaching journey truly commences.

Games offer a powerful platform for teaching cause-and-effect relationships, critical thinking, and strategy. They also emphasize the importance of organization and time management. Teaching not only the skills but when and how to apply them for success is essential.

Our children have lost their understanding of how to behave in large groups, and it's crucial to reteach these skills. When entering a large group setting, we should ask ourselves important questions such as, "What is the group's objective?" and "Why am I here?" Understanding our role within the group is essential—whether we're contributing to the group, gaining from it, or collaborating to achieve a specific task. Knowing these roles helps us determine which skill set to apply. Are we sharing information, absorbing it, or simply working together toward a common goal?

Ideally, as the large group progresses toward its objective, we should find ourselves playing all three roles interchangeably. Teaching "when" and "why" to embrace these roles is vital for the success of everyone involved. This learning process takes time, demanding plenty of practice and thoughtful consideration about our role within the group. It's a dynamic give-and-take among all members, understanding when to contribute and when to receive, a critical aspect for the group's success.

Many individuals within a group aspire to be the center of attention, and this often leads to issues. Some people lack the skill set to differentiate between positive and negative attention. Therefore, we must train our children in this aspect. They need to learn how to distinguish between positive attention, where people appreciate their actions and encourage them, and negative attention, where people want them to cease their behavior. These are basic social cues that our children might have forgotten or never learned, and it's vital to reintroduce them, primarily for their safety.

Over the past year, my wife and I have been devoting our attention to understanding the complex social dynamics our daughters have been facing. It wasn't a matter of possessing some "all-knowing eye," predicting that our kids would require this form of reteaching in the future. Instead, it began with a simple observation—one day, while walking down the hallway, we noticed our youngest daughter in tears. This was unusual because she typically didn't cry without a clear reason. When we asked her what was troubling her, she struggled to articulate her feelings, which deeply concerned us.

In response, we hugged it out, engaged in heartfelt conversations, and made genuine efforts to listen more attentively. Gradually, we uncovered the root of her distress: her friends were embroiled in conflicts characterized by strong personalities vying for dominance. These disputes led to hurt feelings and exclusion, and my daughter was profoundly affected by witnessing her friends' unkind behavior.

Our approach was to lend a sympathetic ear and give her the space to express her emotions. We wished we had all the right answers to immediately resolve the situation, but we understood that we couldn't change other people's actions. What we could control, however, were our own actions and how we guided our daughter. We imparted to her the valuable life lesson that when you're unhappy with how your friends are behaving, it's essential to communicate your concerns. If your friends persist in such behavior despite your efforts, you have the option to distance yourself from them. This is a huge life lesson.

Reteaching life skills and proper behavior in various communities, both large and small, is a vital step in addressing the issues our children face. It boils down to identifying our goals, understanding our skill sets, and integrating them effectively into the community. This approach yields remarkable results. In my experience, I employ a similar method at the outset of every trip with students. The majority respond positively the first time, while some require more time to adapt. With a confident demeanor, a receptive attitude, and supportive guidance, I convey that they're not in trouble; I merely need them to adjust their behavior. This approach works well for about 90-95% of all students on my trips.

Part 3 - Coaching

Coaching represents the purest form of learning. It involves a structured process of studying, acquiring knowledge, practicing skills, understanding when to apply those skills, and ultimately integrating them in real-time situations. The results are immediate and serve as clear feedback on whether one has executed a skill correctly or not. My experience coaching sports significantly contributed to my growth as an educator. The essence of coaching lies in figuring out how to guide a group of individuals, each with varying skill levels, toward achieving a common goal.

To illustrate this concept, let's examine ice hockey. In hockey, I train athletes in various skills such as shooting, skating, passing, hitting, and stick handling. Once they have honed these skills, they are placed in game-like situations where they learn not only when to use these skills but also how to use them effectively. Coaching comes into play when athletes realize that their skills can influence the actions of the opposing team. The better they can utilize their skills to assert control over the game, the greater their chances of winning and achieving their goal.

In the context of our children's lives, they are currently navigating the complexities of a post-COVID-19 world. While many of them have retained some essential skills and teachings, they find themselves in a state of confusion. Most have forgotten significant skill sets, including mental grit and knowledge of what is socially acceptable behavior. As they seek to reintegrate into teams, clubs, and school groups, they are confronted with the challenge of participating in group events, such as school activities, shows, contests, movies, sports events, and concerts. However, they often lack the knowledge or recollection of how to act successfully in these situations.

Our children are reentering the world, and they need coaching to ensure they can thrive independently. As a parent, the coaching occurs before, during and after we enter a new situation. It could be a huge idea like time management. My wife and I coach this every day. We use countdowns, review calendar events, and support our daughters in prioritizing activities. Simple questions and reminders can be helpful, such as, "School starts in 50 minutes. What do you need to do to get ready?" "Tomorrow is busy; you have a game to play, a game to go to, and a dance to attend. When are you going to eat? What are you going to eat?" "Do you have anything you need to do for school? If so, when are you going to do it?" "We have one hour to buy groceries; how can you help me get everything in that time?"

Along with time management, we are coaching how to be a good friend. It involves a lot of listening. We ask things like, "Why are you mad at this person? Is this a final straw or just really annoying?" and "How can you help them understand how you feel? Has this happened with other friends? If so, how did you resolve it?"

Coaching is using the right skills at the right time to get the best results. You have to know which skills you have access to and how to use them together in a real time situation. It is challenging, but when you get it right, it is the difference between a good day and a great day. Having skills and knowing when to use them is the essence of coaching.

Good coaches grow programs, and parents are no different. Good parents know their kids' friends. Good parents use every opportunity to extend their coaching to their kids' friends, fostering a supportive and respectful community.

Taking measured steps is crucial. We have to move with purpose. If you fail to plan then you plan to fail. Skills are gradually linked together to form habits, which, in turn, lead to established courses of action. These actions then transform into plans for achieving goals in real-life situations.

I recently took my oldest daughter and some of her friends to the county fair. I reviewed time management skills. "When are we leaving?" "Where are we meeting?" Then I started to link other skills. "What do you do if you get lost?" "What do you do if your phone is starting to die?" I started giving them fill-in-the blank responses. "Everyone should _____ together! Don't_____ the fairgrounds." Lastly, "if there's an emergency and we have to evacuate the fair, meet back near the entrance."

I stayed at the fair and texted them every couple of hours. They updated me about their progress. I had reviewed skill sets, linked them together, and sent my daughter and her friends into the fair. They had boundaries and freedom. I would use this same format at a mall, high school game, or amusement park. I would do each slightly differently, but this is how I would base my training.

As parents, we naturally engage in this process of coaching every day. Now we have the chance to revisit and reinforce these major concepts and values, applying them to various situations and doing so consistently across the board. Let's bring this all together by working through a couple of examples.

Example One: Rebuilding Our Family Group

The impact of COVID-19 was profound on my family. It took a toll on my wife, my daughters, and myself. I found myself battling depression, my wife was filled with worry, and my daughters seemed stuck to the couch, disconnected from the world. Recognizing that we all needed to regain our sense of vitality, I set a goal: to rekindle family togetherness through enjoyable activities. It was the classic "forced family fun," and my initial attempts at this during the first three weeks of the summer ended in failure. My wife helped me see why – I had been focusing on what I wanted rather than what everyone needed.

The turning point came when my youngest daughter proposed the idea of a game night. Although I didn't sit down to create a structured plan, I had a clear vision of what I wanted to achieve with game night. Fortunately, my wife and I had experience with game nights over the past 15 years, which allowed us to embark on this endeavor with some proficiency.

Skills involved in this process:

1. **Teamwork**: To motivate everyone to embrace change.
2. **Fun**: Making activities enjoyable to encourage participation.
3. **Peer pressure**: Encouraging reluctant family members to get involved.
4. **Time management**: Ensuring activities start and end at the right times to keep them enjoyable.
5. **Manners**: Promoting respectful behavior to build a sense of unity.
6. **The "Golden Rule"**: Emphasizing the importance of making everyone feel valued by treating them how you would want to be treated.
7. **Communication**: Fostering the ability to convey ideas and minimize frustration.
8. **Listening skills**: Understanding the wants and needs of all family members to facilitate compromise when necessary.
9. **Sportsmanship (Mental Toughness)**: Instilling the importance of gracious behavior, whether winning or losing, and the willingness to try again to improve results.

This list is by no means exhaustive, as the possibilities for skills to teach are endless. However, it's essential to prioritize and focus on the skills that matter most to your family's specific goals. Once these fundamental skills are relearned and ingrained, you can expand to include more.

In terms of teaching, it's important to remember that the game itself is merely the backdrop for the lessons you want to impart. Consider this a "teachable moment." Preparing for this moment takes time and thought. I had been contemplating this for weeks, recognizing that my kids needed motivation to engage with the world, have adventures, spend time with friends, reconnect with family, and join new communities. They also needed to comprehend their environment and apply their skills to achieve their goals, all of which came into play during our game nights.

Outline of the Teaching Process:

1. **Learning the game**: Initially, teaching the rules and mechanics of the game.
2. **Strategic thinking:** Moving beyond the basics to teach how to strategize and compete with others to achieve success. This is where you remove the training wheels and allow them to experience failure as a learning opportunity, rather than a chance for verbal or emotional abuse. Remember, the purpose of playing is to learn and have fun, not to face criticism.
3. **Fostering presence in the moment:** Disconnecting from screens and phones and encouraging the family to enjoy each other's company
4. **Observational skills:** Developing the ability to observe and appreciate each other's moves, recognizing their knowledge and growth.
5. **Modeling behavior:** Leading by example in terms of manners, attitude, grit, respect for good moves, and showing empathy when someone faces setbacks.

Ultimately, using the game as a tool to reteach valuable life skills and appropriate conduct.

This holistic approach helps not only to rebuild family bonds but also to equip your children with essential life skills that extend far beyond the game night itself. This can be used with any game.

One of the great aspects of card games is the opportunity for reflection after each hand. We discussed how we played and whether we could have done better. This allowed us to teach important concepts like cause-and-effect relationships and risk-reward behavior. Furthermore, our children were learning how their actions influenced the group. They could celebrate their own successes and analyze their failures in a close-knit setting.

Coaching moments in the game:

Coaching is preparing for the real time application of skills sets and strategies. Coaching played a vital role in this experience. It involved applying real-life skills and goals to the game, considering the results, and striving to improve in subsequent rounds. We analyzed cause-and-effect relationships, seeking to understand how actions could influence other players. For instance, we discussed strategies for handling trump cards, protecting them, exposing them, or using weaker trump cards strategically.

Coaching is built upon a wealth of experience, whether gained directly or indirectly. Fables, for example, have long been used to coach children through life's challenges. While the games themselves were important, my primary motivation for initiating these family activities was to build trust with our daughters and create an environment where they felt comfortable sharing their fears and anxieties. Throughout the game nights, I remained attentive, waiting for the right moment to connect with our daughters on a deeper level.

The key moment came when they began opening up about their conflicts and emotions. This was the crucial breakthrough we had been working toward. We had created a diversion—a shared goal, happiness, and a safe space—that allowed us to trust each other with our problems. By creating this safety, we were addressing step two on Maslow's hierarchy, laying the foundation for the third step in our community. We were constructing an emotional community characterized by empathy and care.

Active listening was crucial during these conversations. We inquired about their thoughts and plans, offering praise or advice as needed. Sometimes, all they needed was someone to listen and empathize. Healing often comes from sharing rather than finding a solution.

As the game nights continued, we gained insight into our daughters' challenges, which were predominantly social in nature. They were dealing with the complexities of friendships, the discomfort of conflicts among friends, and other sources of stress and frustration. Game night remains a cherished tradition for our family.

Example Two: Working with Large Groups

The pandemic brought about a prolonged shutdown of large group activities, and as a result, our children have forgotten how to act in such settings. In my daily work with large groups, I've observed that I need to constantly retrain, reteach, and coach students to reacquire these essential skills. The impact of the pandemic has been felt not only in educational settings but also in various public venues, such as concert and movie theaters, where people seem to have forgotten how to behave in large groups.

To retrain students for success in groups, I begin with a set of fundamental rules:

1. **Listening**: Pay attention to what's being said.
2. **Following Directions**: Do as instructed.
3. **Looking at the Teacher**: Maintain visual focus.
4. **Raising Your Hand**: Use this to speak or participate.
5. **Listening When Your Peers Are Talking**: Respect others' voices.
6. **No Screaming:** Unless it's a 911 emergency, keep noise levels appropriate.
7. **Hands and Voice to Yourself**: Avoid disrupting others.
8. **No Running or Throwing Things**: Promote safety.
9. **Have Fun**: Enjoy the experience.

I spend considerable time reviewing and reinforcing these rules at the beginning of each trip, making the process engaging and interactive. This can involve activities like calling out numbers, sharing stories, seeking student input, and generally keeping the students engaged and interested.

Once these fundamental skills are reestablished, I can move on to reteaching how a large group operates. Some of the main themes I focus on include:

1. **Trust**: Emphasizing that trust is essential for group activities. Without trust, we cannot engage in riskier or more enjoyable activities as a group.

2. **Time Management**: Highlighting that following the rules efficiently allows us to make the most of our time together. This could involve discussing how adhering to guidelines ensures we can participate in more activities.

3. **Taking Care of Our Stuff**: Encouraging students to be responsible for the equipment and resources we use during our group activities and reinforcing the importance of respect for shared resources.

4. **Incorporating Learning**: Integrating educational aspects like science and history into our activities throughout the day. This helps students understand that, even while having fun, they can learn and grow.

In this way, we gradually rebuild the skills and understanding necessary for effective participation in large groups. It's a process that requires patience, persistence, and a focus on both behavioral and educational development.

Working with students in large groups is a constantly evolving challenge, and retraining, teaching, and coaching are vital components of helping them develop essential life skills. From addressing issues like inappropriate behavior during lunch to dealing with disruptive screaming, it's clear that guiding students toward appropriate conduct is an ongoing process.

The hard skills are the easy part. Listening, raising your hand, not calling out, sharing, and cleaning up are hard skills. They are necessary to complete the work and are usually easy to spot and retrain. The soft skills are personal qualities and impact how you work. Soft skills include how to interact with people when you disagree, persistence, and mental toughness (Long).

These soft skills are a lot harder to access, see, and address. These skills are usually hidden while the group is sitting quietly and listening. They tend to show themselves when the students get to work in small groups. Unpacking conflicts and figuring out what skills need to be addressed is a lot harder and takes time to work out.

Part 4 - Concluding Thoughts

Retraining is the reinforcement of skills and skill sets, from the simple saying "please" and "thank you" to the more complex getting ready for bed or being a good friend. Reteaching is connecting these skills with the cause and effect on your environment. If the skill is sharing, teaching involves understanding how sharing affects our community. We share to build trust and strengthen our community. If the skill set is showing people respect, the teaching is showing the effect of this skill set on the people we interact with. We treat people with respect because that shows we value them. When people feel valued, they tend to be more engaged in activities and help more. The teaching expands on the skill set to show examples of completing complicated projects by breaking them into smaller parts. Examples and strategies are linked to success and failure.

Coaching involves reflecting on past experiences, understanding cause and effect, and developing strategies to achieve goals. It involves accessing previous skill sets and strategies and applying them to a new environment with praise and reflection. Coaching also provides another chance. Failure is okay if you learn from it. We all fail; no one was born knowing how to do everything. Coaching allows for continuous improvement and helps students adapt to different situations effectively. It involves respect and the belief that you can be successful if you practice and work hard.

As parents, teachers, and mentors, our role is multifaceted. We must train, teach, and coach our children to equip them with the skills, knowledge, and abilities needed to navigate various environments successfully. Collaboration with other parents and seeking guidance from experienced mentors and coaches can provide valuable insights and support in this journey.

Now is the time to focus on nurturing our children's motivational needs, fostering their personal development, and enhancing their cognitive skills. Our guidance and support are essential as they continue to grow, learn and rebuild their communities. We are our children's first teachers and coaches. We trained them from the beginning. We taught them how to deal with this world. We brought them to their first playgrounds. We formed their first communities.

Now is the time to fire the social media substitute. We need to move with purpose. We need to coach our children as they rediscover all the lost playgrounds and seek out new ones. Now is the time to become our children's best teachers and coaches.

Let's rediscover old playgrounds and find new ones. Let's make our communities stronger. Let's move with purpose!

Acknowledgements

While I have always dreamed of writing a book, this is not the book that I dreamed about writing. This book came out of nowhere and swallowed me whole. I have been all in since the idea came to me. Writing this book has been exciting from the start. It has been a form of therapy for me, a gift to myself and my family. This book has helped me organize and process my trials and tribulations. A book like this takes a community to write. My community grew as the book did, and they all made it possible. Their excitement was contagious and pushed me through the hard parts.

I have to start by thanking my wife, Kelli. She is my co-trainer, my co-teacher, and my co-coach. We talk, brainstorm, and work together to build our family. It is great having a partner you trust working with you. She has given me time and space to finish this project and has helped with ideas and support along the way. She even did the title artwork on the cover. Thank you, Kelli, for all of your love and support. I love you Madly.

My daughters, Lauren and Claire, played my reindeer games all summer. They let me interview them and pick their brains for ideas. This book would not have been possible without them. Claire also helped me design and create the cover art. She made all the bowling pins. Thank you both.

A book is nothing without an editor; my niece, Megan McIntosh, took ownership of this mantel. Thank you for believing in this book enough to edit it. Your insight and ideas have grown this project, and I really appreciate all your advice. Thank you for all the ideas to improve this story and all the compliments that kept me excited about the idea.

Vicki Quist is my mother-in-law, and I admire her strength, courage, and attention to detail. When I had my book finished, I asked her if she would be willing to give her feedback. She agreed and took to the task with all the respect and care of my own mother. Thank you for your insight and attention to my words. I am forever grateful

I also want to thank my friend Andrew Wiley. We talked for a long time in the summer, and our conversation convinced me that other people would like to hear this story. Thank you for your help and guidance along the way.

Dr. Justin LaPilusa, PSY.D. is the mastermind for the idea of Chapter 9. We talked for an hour about the book, and he directed me to dive into the psychosocial development of our kids. While this chapter was a bear to write, it really helped me make connections. Thank you for listening, believing, and seeing the value in exploring how our kids develop. Your insight into major theories and your attention to the details in how I presented the material was inspiring. Thank you for taking the time to help me focus my message and dial in my voice.

I would also like to thank Tanya Trazi, APRN for her help with Chapter 9 as well. Thank you for taking the time to look over my work. Proofreading a crazy friend's ideas out of the blue is a huge ask, and you jumped aboard with excitement. Having you look over my writing was a great gift, and I truly appreciate you taking the time.

I would also like to thank my boss, Brett Querry, and my coworkers, Troy Carter and Tony Freeman. Our conversations at the end of the day helped me refine my teaching strategies and understand my students a little better.

Lastly, I would like to thank you, the reader. Thank you for making time to explore these ideas. I hope that you found the book as exciting to read as I found it exciting to write. I hope my book gives you hope and motivation to start moving with purpose, to start discovering new playgrounds, to start building your communities and making them stronger.

Acknowledgments

278

Works Cited

Buffett, Jimmy. "Mental Floss." Banana Wind, 1996, Track 9.

Cherry, Kendra. "Erikson's Stages of Development: A Closer Look at the Eight Psychosocial Stages." *Verywell Mind*, 3 Aug. 2022, www.verywellmind.com/erik-eriksons-stages-of-psychosocial-development-2795740

Finding Nemo. Directed by Andrew Stanton, Pixar Animation Studios / Walt Disney Pictures, 2003.

Germin, Brian. "Best Fear Quotes by Brian Germain." *Best Fear Quotes*, www.transcendingfear.com/quotes-brian.html.

Goodkind, Terry. "Chapter 46." *Faith of the Fallen*, Tor Fantasy, New York, New York, 2000, pp. 520–525.

Groundhog Day. Directed by Harold Ramis, Columbia Pictures, 1993.

Hannah Gadsby: Nanette. Directed by Madeleine Parry and Jon Olb, written by Hannah Gadsby, Guesswork Televison, 2018.

Herring, Tiana. "The Research Is Clear: Solitary Confinement Causes Long-Lasting Harm." *Prison Policy Initiative*, 8 Dec. 2020, www.prisonpolicy.org/blog/2020/12/08/solitary_symposium/.

Long, Brita. "Hard Skills vs. Soft Skills: What Are They? (With Examples)." *InsightGlobal*, 16 Aug. 2022, insightglobal.com/blog/hard-skills-vs-soft-skills/.

"Solitary Confinement Facts." *American Friends Service Committee*, afsc.org/solitary-confinement-facts.

Mary Poppins. Directed by Robert Stevenson, Walt Disney Pictures, 1964.

Mcleod, Saul. "Erik Erikson's Stages of Psychosocial Development." *Simply Psychology*, 16 Oct. 2023, www.simplypsychology.org/erik-erikson.html.

Mcleod, Saul. "Maslow's Hierarchy of Needs." *Simply Psychology*, 24 Oct. 2023, www.simplypsychology.org/maslow.html.

Mcleod, Saul. "Piaget's Theory and Stages of Cognitive Development." *Simply Psychology*, 24 Oct. 2023, www.simplypsychology.org/piaget.html.

Rowling, J. K., et al. *Harry Potter and the Sorcerer's Stone.* Arthur A. Levine Books, 2015.

Shrek. Directed by Andrew Adamson and Vicky Jenson, DreamWorks Pictures / DreamWorks Animation / Pacific Data Images, 2001.

Smith, William. "Piaget's Schema & Learning Theory: 3 Fascinating Experiments." *PositivePsychology.Com*, 13 Oct. 2023, positivepsychology.com/piaget-schemas/#examples.

"Stages of Human Development: What It Is & Why It's Important." *Maryville University Online*, 11 Oct. 2023, online.maryville.edu/online-bachelors-degrees/human-development-and-family-studies/resources/stages-of-human-development/#stages-human-development.

"Stress." *World Health Organization*, 21 Feb. 2023, https://www.who.int/news-room/questions-and-answers/item/stress.

Sus, Viktoriya. "Industry vs Inferiority: 10 Examples (Erikson 4th Stage)." Edited by Chris Drew, *Helpful Professor*, 18 Apr. 2023, helpfulprofessor.com/industry-vs-inferiority-examples/.

"The CDC Says Teen Mental Health Is in Crisis. Who Is Most at Risk?" *USAFacts*, 4 Oct. 2023, usafacts.org/articles/the-cdc-says-teen-mental-health-is-in-crisis-who-is-most-at-risk/

Zhou, Molly, and David Brown. "Psychosocial Theory of Identity Development." Dalton State University Educational Learning Theories, LibreTexts, Davis, CA, 2023, p. 8.1-8.2.6.

Made in United States
Orlando, FL
07 December 2023

40346285R00153